ALSO BY STEPHEN E. AMBROSE

THE VICTORS:
Eisenhower and His Boys: The Men of World War II

AMERICANS AT WAR

CITIZEN SOLDIERS:
The U.S. Army from the Normandy Beaches to the Bulge to the Surrender of Germany, June 7, 1944–May 7, 1945

UNDAUNTED COURAGE:
Meriwether Lewis, Thomas Jefferson, and the Opening of the American West

D-DAY:
June 6, 1944: The Climactic Battle of World War II

BAND OF BROTHERS:
E Company, 506th Regiment, 101st Airborne from Normandy to Hitler's Eagle's Nest

NIXON:
Ruin and Recovery, 1973–1990

EISENHOWER:
Soldier and President

NIXON:
The Triumph of a Politician, 1962–1972

NIXON:
The Education of a Politician, 1913–1962

PEGASUS BRIDGE: June 6, 1944

EISENHOWER:
The President

EISENHOWER:
Soldier, General of the Army, President-Elect, 1890–1952

THE SUPREME COMMANDER:
The War Years of General Dwight D. Eisenhower

DUTY, HONOR, COUNTRY:
A History of West Point

EISENHOWER AND BERLIN, 1945

CRAZY HORSE AND CUSTER:
The Parallel Lives of Two American Warriors

RISE TO GLOBALISM:
American Foreign Policy, 1938–1992

IKE'S SPIES:
Eisenhower and the Espionage Establishment

HALLECK: Lincoln's Chief of Staff

UPTON AND THE ARMY

COMRADES

BROTHERS,

FATHERS,

HEROES,

SONS,

PALS

Stephen E. Ambrose

Illustrations by Jon Friedman

SIMON & SCHUSTER

SIMON & SCHUSTER
Rockefeller Center
1230 Avenue of the Americas
New York, NY 10020

Copyright © 1999 by Ambrose-Tubbs, Inc.

Illustrations © 1999 by Jon Friedman

All rights reserved,
including the right of reproduction
in whole or in part in any form.
SIMON & SCHUSTER and colophon are
registered trademarks of Simon & Schuster Inc.
Designed by Edith Fowler
Manufactured in the United States of America

10   9   8   7   6   5   4   3   2   1

Library of Congress Cataloging-in-Publication Data
is available.
ISBN 0-684-86718-4

Contents

For Harry and Bill

Introduction

ONE OF THE JOYS of my adult life has been discovering male friendships. I have written about many male relationships, and I thought to draw on them for a small book on the subject of friendship. It had occurred to me that this subject is seldom discussed, nothing to the extent that sexual, family, and business relationships are examined. We have an endless number of books on how to have better sex, exercise better, eat better, lose weight, drive better, speak well in public and so on.

Friendship among men is difficult for Anglo-Saxon males of a middle-class background to define or practice. I was well into my fifties before I discovered the pleasure of hugging a male friend. Now I do it habitually. Often, and always with my brothers, I have to initiate it. It embarrasses them, but they can't refuse. General Dwight Eisenhower wrote at the end of his life that he regretted his inability to give hugs to his fellows. Men are also reluctant to "spill their guts out" (Richard Nixon's words), even to a close friend. They don't like to show emotion. Yet we'll meet here a number of men who overcame their inhibitions and developed deep, lasting, engaging, rewarding friendships.

For some of these pieces I reread pages or chapters from

my writings that speak to such friendships. I confess that I enjoy going back to read my old books, where I meet old friends. I selected passages that illuminate particular friendships. It is a broad list, stretching from Lewis and Clark to the present day and including young friends, middle-aged friends, and old friends. It includes men who achieved the highest level of friendship fighting together in war.

I start with my brothers, one older and one younger, men with whom I've had the longest and deepest friendship, and conclude with my father, my model. I write about a hero of mine, Dwight Eisenhower, who along with his brother Milton and his fellow Army officer George S. Patton were men I "met" doing research. Then there are Custer and his brothers, Crazy Horse and He Dog, Lewis and Clark, along with the men of Easy Company, 506th Parachute Infantry Regiment, 101st Airborne Division, and three old war veterans Hans von Luck, John Howard and Dick Winters.

What's most important to me about writing is the learning along the way. After years of researching these and other men, I knew that the only way I could satisfy my curiosity was to write about them. I have learned a lot about friendship, from both these men and my own friends, who have a talent for it. This is especially true of the two explorers Lewis and Clark, and in the twentieth century, of Dwight Eisenhower. Ike had more friends than anybody else because he was so congenial, outgoing, curious and respectful. He was a man who loved life and who loved people. In this regard he was the opposite of Richard Nixon, which is the reason I've included a chapter on why Nixon found it so difficult to make friends.

After that I started to write about my own friends. Writing is never fun, but thinking about my friends is. I have many more I have not written about (my apologies), but the guys in these essays are dear to me in special ways. The

friends of one's birth, siblings, offer the security of identification and utter familiarity. School friends bring early gifts
—imagination, tolerance, a new kind of fun. The friends
of one's adulthood offer support, steadfastness and unques-
tioned, if tough, love. The friends one meets in work bring
knowledge, openness and acceptance.

Friends come in all different styles, ages, personalities
and habits; we relate to each one differently. You can go days,
months, years without seeing a friend, and resume the relationship with ease. Loving a woman is wholly different. It is
intimate, all-encompassing, and I cannot do without it. But
friends bring much else I would not have otherwise.

As I wrote this book I learned what a wide bunch of
friends I have. I've had my imagination stirred, my tolerance
expanded. I've learned a lot. I've had a lot of fun.

The four best words in the English language are love,
wife, home and work. The fifth one is friend. Here are some
of mine, past and present.

ONE

Brothers:
The Ambrose Boys

WE WERE YOUNG TOGETHER, we grew up together in White-water, Wisconsin, we have known each other longer than we have known anyone else except our parents. I can tell you without having to look whether Harry will hit a fastball or a curve or a change-up, or whether Bill will make a hook or a set shot or a left-handed layup. And they can tell you what I can and can't do on a tennis court, a football field or a basketball floor. And what else? What magazines they will read, or newspapers. What clothes will appeal. Most of all, in our younger days, what girls would appeal to them, and who their friends would be. Such knowledge just is.

Harry is two years older than I, Bill two years younger. We didn't feel much like a band of brothers when we were kids, except on the high school sports teams, mainly because our mother began goading us into competition over the breakfast table and carried it on until bedtime. When we were in grade school, the competition was over who could run or swim the fastest or farthest, or climb the highest tree, or hike the hills or gather the most wood for the woodstove at the cabin. When we were in our teens, it was over grades, courses and sports.

By then, however, we needed no goading. A very big

part of my life was catching up to and surpassing Harry, while keeping Bill well back from me. Each of us constantly challenged the other two, especially in sports. We had a basketball backboard and goal over the garage, where we played one-on-one with great intensity, getting into the most terrific arguments over who had fouled whom. In that driveway, we would use tennis balls to play one-on-one baseball. I would pitch while Harry or Bill batted, using the garage doors for a backstop. Hit the ball so far for a single, thus far for a double, and so on, with loud discussions about who was pitching fair and who was not and how far a ball that had been hit had gone, or disagreements about what was a ball and what was a strike.

Worst was the golf course, when we were in high school, because we knew each other so well that we could pick the exact moment for a little cough on the putting green, just enough to break a brother's concentration at the instant he was going to stroke the ball, but so soft and apparently irrepressible that he could not legitimately complain.

What made the competition bearable was that we played together on the high school football, basketball and track teams. As a senior, Harry was the quarterback of the football team, on which I was the guard and linebacker, and we played well together. Our team lost one game and was conference champion, which gave us great pride and prestige and a fierce defensiveness of each other. We were not so good in basketball—too short and too slow—and no good at all in track, but we supported and stood up for each other. Bill was O.K. in football and basketball, so we played pickup with him when it was necessary.

We talked about our parents, nearly always or so it seems now. We thought Mother was much too talkative, far too inclined to rat on us to our dad, had too many friends and spent far too much time with them, and suffered other shortcomings, but we also thought she was a natural for the county board and the school board and anything else she might choose to run for. As for Dad, a doctor in town, we agreed that for his patients and friends he was easily the best man in town, but for us he was far too demanding and much too inclined to yell and spank, but we were very glad that he was our father. We wouldn't have traded him for anyone else.

Mainly, we knew which of us was best at mowing the lawn or shoveling the walks or weeding the garden (best meant being able to do the job well enough to almost satisfy Dad), which girl in the other guy's high school class had a reputation for putting out and who she went out with (never with us, it seemed), which students were best in Latin or algebra, and so on and on and on. If we didn't know who had gotten an A in third-year Latin or fourth-year typing, Mother would make sure we were informed—she was as competitive as our dad.

When time came for us to go to college, we were competing against our peers rather than each other. Harry took a national test and did well enough to get a scholarship through Navy ROTC to go to Dartmouth. He was terribly set up to be at an Ivy League school and remains so today. For our part, Bill and I thought it all rather a lot of foolishness. I went to the University of Wisconsin on a football scholarship. Bill followed me to Madison on his own money, made on summer jobs. Harry sneered at us for being at the state university, while we sneered at him for being at Dartmouth.

After college, they both spent time in the service—Harry as a lieutenant in the Marine Corps, Bill as a lieutenant in the Navy. The Cold War had no active battles going on after President Dwight Eisenhower shut down the Korean War, so I thought they were crazy and quit the ROTC. After serving their two or three years, they both went to business school for their MBA and then into real work, while I went to graduate school and then into teaching. Harry rose to a senior position in a major firm in the commodities market; Bill spent considerable time with Corning Glass before becoming owner and operator of a furniture factory in Maine.

Harry's work was hectic, stressful and demanding. Bill's work after he left Corning Glass was on the furniture shop floor, ankle-deep in sawdust, doing for a living what Dad had done as a hobby, making Harry and me exceedingly proud of him. Harry was at the cutting edge of technology in the corn and grain market; Bill was operating a factory that differed from a Maine furniture factory of the nineteenth century only in having electricity to power the tools in place of waterpower. Harry's work took him to many different cities for varying lengths of time; Bill has been in Maine ever since acquiring the factory.

My own work was as a scholar and teacher, and I never made as much money as my brothers, but I did make enough to take the summers off and go out west with my wife and children. They envied me for the time I spent with my family; I envied them for the money they made. None of us would have traded with one another.

We got together at least once a year, usually more often, most of all at the family cabin in northern Wisconsin in August, beloved by all of us. Then there are family weddings, funerals, celebrations and reunions. It was in Whitewater on one such occasion, shortly after our mother died, at a formal dinner honoring our father, that he said our all-time favorite comment about us. Each of us had said something about Dad's decades of service to the community and how proud of him we were. It was the kind of thing we could never say to him in private, as it would have been far too embarrassing. He was a man who praised sparingly, if ever. He had always let us know when he was dissatisfied. None of us had ever done our assigned tasks to his standard. When we did begin to mow the lawn right or shovel the snow, the only way we knew it was that Dad didn't send us out to do it again.

That night, however, with his sons standing beside him, he told his friends and neighbors, "I want you to know that if my boys are proud of me, no one will ever know how proud I am of them."

By God, that was a moment! To be cherished, always. He did it just right. The praise was for all of us, we brothers, we band of three.

He expressed not only his love and admiration for us but also pushed aside the competitiveness that had characterized our relationship with each other—all three sons were equal in his love, which is what mattered. This was a turning point in our relationships with each other that bonded us forever in a new, mature way. Decades of intense competition in sports, school and for our parents' praise and attention, plus a severe break caused by a war, had given way to tolerance, openness, sharing and mutual admiration.

Wherever our careers have taken us, and it has been to many different places, we have always kept up with and been exceedingly proud of each other, and never hesitated to say so. We have turned out quite differently, one from another, but our experiences as members of the same family have created a unique bond. When we get together today, our competition comes back pretty strong, especially when we are hiking, golfing or playing tennis. We revert to the way we acted and talked when we were teenagers. We call each other by our childhood nicknames.

Harry plays the older brother, forever showing us the way. He tells me what the subject of my next book should be. He tells Bill how to make furniture. He tells us where we should vacation and what IRAs to buy, and so on. And he is forever explaining politics to me. His heart is good and he can't help himself, so Bill and I nod yes to everything he says and never do any of it.

There was a time in the late sixties and early seventies when that trust and affection were put to a painful test. It was during the Vietnam War. Harry was vociferously in support of the war, Bill quietly in support, I loudly opposed. The war tore us apart as it did the country. Never since the Civil War, which I have studied and written about, have we Americans felt so estranged from one another, and this extended into every family in the nation. I was not able to understand how my brothers could be hawks, just as they couldn't understand me. It was just terrible. I was unable to talk to them on the telephone, much less see them.

The war ended, finally, and gradually we began to reestablish communications, primarily thanks to our wives and kids. There was at first a stiffness to our relationship, but at least we were talking. We had learned never to bring up politics, but even that prohibition eventually broke down. I recall a two-hour telephone conversation with Harry the night before the 1980 election (I told him he couldn't possibly vote for an actor for president; he said the same about the current president). Then in the mid-eighties, we brothers had a discussion about families and finances. One of us had a friend whose brother was a drunk, wife-beater, the works. In addition to the embarrassment, the friend carried a heavy financial burden to support his brother's family. We talked about how lucky we were that such a situation had never intruded in our lives. Indeed, we agreed, it was a source of great comfort to us to know that not only would we not be called upon to bail out one of us, but we could count on the other brothers if we ever needed help, no questions asked.

The best times come today at the August gathering in northern Wisconsin, three generations worth. Grandchildren swimming and laughing, diving and splashing, as many as a dozen of them, northwoods bike rides and canoe adventures, golf and tennis, campfires. Our wives all get along just fine; our children are very close, they love to be together. Harry, Bill and I sit on the porch and talk about our parents—we seem to remember only the good things, what they did for us, anecdotes about their card games or trips together—and we talk about Whitewater in that long-ago time and our high school friends, about games we played with each other and against each other, and then back to Dad and Mom, always the prime subject.

We recall the typing class, or our Latin teacher, or mowing the lawn, or doing the dishes, and as best we can we express our conviction that this was the best thing that ever happened to us, that without their prodding we would never be where we are now. And if one of us should happen to bring up what Dad said about us at the dinner in his honor, why then the tears are sure to follow.

That moment bonded us forever in a new, grown-up way. As adults, in the wake of disappointment, there is tolerance and openness and sharing.

TWO

Brothers:
The Eisenhower Boys

OF ALL THE FRIENDSHIPS between brothers that I've known, and there have been many, none came close to that of the six Eisenhower boys. Partly that was because of their parents, partly because of their semi-rural setting, partly because there were so many of them and they had no sisters, partly it was because of their personalities. They had learned from David and Ida Eisenhower always to love one another, other people and every manifestation of life around them. They grew up without money or any possessions, only each other. And although they had some friends in the little town of Abilene, Kansas, where they lived, mainly they had to rely on each other.

Dwight Eisenhower was born on October 14, 1890, into a working-class family that already had two sons, Arthur born in 1886 and Edgar born in January 1889. Roy was born in 1892, Paul in 1894 (he died in infancy), Earl in 1898 and Milton in 1899. "I have found out in later years we were very poor," Dwight Eisenhower said in a 1952 speech that kicked off his campaign for U.S. president, "but the glory of America is that we didn't know it then. All that we knew was that our parents—of great courage—could say to us: Opportunity is all about you. Reach out and take it."

David worked in the local creamery; the boys had their own patch of ground to grow vegetables, which they sold around town; their mother, Ida, was universally regarded as a saint. Neither parent ever smoked, drank or swore, or raised their voices—although all their boys did. One of Dwight's sharpest memories about his father concerned the day that his father came home early for lunch and discovered that Edgar had been skipping school to work at a part-time job. He grabbed Edgar by the collar and started whipping him. Dwight, then twelve years old, shouted at his father to stop. That didn't work, so he came up behind his father and grabbed his arms.

"Oh, do you want some of the same? What's the matter with you, anyway?"

"I don't think anyone ought to be whipped like that," Dwight sobbed, "not even a dog." David dropped his strap, turned away and stormed off. Years later, telling the story, Dwight insisted that the punishment was deserved and beneficial: "Had it not been for the application of leather," he said, "prolonged and unforgettable, my brother might well have become an unhappy handyman in Kansas."

In a family of six boys, competition was the natural order of things—racing, climbing, grades in classes, everything, including fighting. "There was no animosity in our fights," Edgar later said. "We fought for the sheer joy of slugging one another. We had to get rid of our energy and I think that when a fight was over we probably thought more of one another than we did before it began."

This was not a time when average Americans took graduating from high school for granted. Two years before his class graduated, Arthur left school to find work in a bank in Kansas City, where he lived in a boardinghouse with Harry S. Truman, and eventually went on to become president of the biggest bank in the city. Edgar also dropped out of school after his sophomore year and eventually became a lawyer; Roy, another dropout, became a druggist in Junction City, Kansas; Earl an engineer in Pennsylvania.

Dwight and Milton stayed in school, where each one did well. Dwight graduated in 1911 and accepted an appointment to West Point. The day he left to become a soldier, Milton told him later, was the first time in his life he had ever heard their mother cry. Milton went on to college and became a journalist. The two men became the closest friends of all the Eisenhower boys, despite their nearly ten-year age difference. In 1926, when the boys gathered in Abilene for a family reunion, each was healthy, alert and getting ahead in his career—although it must be said that Dwight was still a major with no prospects, while Milton was the number-two official in the U.S. Agriculture Department.

Dwight, a 1915 graduate of West Point, had nevertheless missed World War I, spending the war as commander of an experimental tank outfit stationed in Gettysburg, Pennsylvania, something he regarded as shameful. He stayed in the Army anyway and in the twenties got posted as aide to General Jack Pershing, the commander of the American Expeditionary Forces in Europe, with an assignment to write a history of American participation in the Great War. He and his wife, Mamie Doud from Denver, found a place to live in the Wyoming Apartments on Connecticut Avenue near Rock Creek Park, with Milton and his wife, Helen, as neighbors. Milton was well known around town as a rising star. His special talent was journalism and he helped his brother put the history together.

It was Dwight's initial tour of duty in Washington, and thus his introduction to a world in which American politics was the almost exclusive subject of conversation. Milton was an excellent guide to that world. Dwight found himself drawn into serious political discussion for the first time in his life and discovered in the process that he was far more conservative than Milton. His brother was chiefly concerned with what the government could do for the people. Dwight, in both their theoretical and practical discussions, found that he put the emphasis on the duty of citizens toward the government. In general, Milton saw a positive role for government and wanted it to grow, while Dwight saw a negative role and wanted it to shrink.

These were differences of degree, not kind. The brothers were similar in many ways. Both loved a good game of bridge, as did their wives, and they frequently played together. They looked alike, with the same big grin and hearty laugh, although Dwight was leaner in the face, tougher in the body. Their voices were so similar that, practical jokers both, they would call the other man's wife on the telephone and carry on a conversation, pretending to be each other. The wives never caught on.

Milton, who had married a wealthy woman whose father was generous with his money, could afford to entertain frequently. Cabinet members, other bureaucrats, Washington lawyers and the Washington press club were his regular guests. Dwight and Mamie joined in the fun. To Milton's delight, Dwight became known in Washington as Milton's brother. At one party, as a reporter was leaving, Milton stopped him and said, "Please don't go until you've met my brother; he's a major in the Army and I know he's going places." Shaking hands with thirty-seven-year-old Major Eisenhower, the reporter thought, If he's going far he had better start soon. But the firm handshake, the lopsided grin and the complete concentration of Eisenhower's blue eyes impressed the reporter. He decided Milton might be right.

By 1939, Dwight Eisenhower was in the Philippines as an assistant to General Douglas MacArthur. He felt he was getting no place in the Army and would be retired as a colonel in the next year or so. Milton, meanwhile, had been offered a position as a dean at Penn State College and wrote his older brother to ask his advice. Dwight typed out a three-page, single-spaced reply. He thought Milton should take the job because of security. As a dean, Milton would have tenure, and the security it brought "is vastly important." Even though Milton was Secretary of Agriculture Henry Wallace's chief assistant in the department and one of the top bureaucrats in Washington, his job had no future.

A major drawback to working for the government, Dwight wrote, was the "driving, continuous mental endeavor" involved. "Men of ability in the government service see so much to be done, they create so many jobs that lazier men like to shunt from their own shoulders that gradually the victim loses his sense of values, and applies his mind, consciously and unconsciously, day and night, to important and intricate problems that march up ceaselessly for consideration." The result of years of such activity, much of which was little more than shuffling paper, "will be a steady, swift grind until you've definitely damaged your own capacity for enjoying life."

Dwight used that line to spring into a discussion of happiness, "Only a man that is happy in his work can be happy in his home, and with his friends," he wrote. "Happiness in work means that its performer must know it to be worthwhile; suited to his temperament, and, finally, suited to his age, experience, and capacity for performance of a high order."

A major advantage to the Penn State offer, Dwight felt, was "freedom in self-expression. The prohibitions, legal and ethical, surrounding the public servant might be largely removed" if Milton became a dean. To be able to speak and write "what you *believe,* not what administration policy supports," struck Dwight as "a tremendous advantage." But Milton rejected the advice, just as Dwight himself, having made an excellent case for his own resignation and a start on a new career, never seriously considered actually doing it.

In September 1939, Hitler invaded Poland and the Second World War in Europe began. To Dwight, although war would mean advancement in his own career and he had dedicated his life to preparing for this challenge, the coming of the conflict was a disaster. On the day war was declared, September 3, he wrote Milton, "After months and months of feverish effort to appease and placate the mad man that is governing Germany, the British and French seem to be driven into a corner out of which they can work their way only by fighting. It's a sad day for Europe and for the whole civilized world—though for a long time it has seemed ridiculous to refer to the world as civilized. If the war is long drawn out and bloody then I believe that the remnants of nations emerging from it will be scarcely recognizable as the ones that entered it." He predicted that "the areas that witness any amount of fighting" would emerge from it cursed by Communism, anarchy, crime and disorder, loss of personal liberty and abject poverty. He blamed Hitler, a "power-drunk egocentric . . . one of the criminally insane . . . the absolute ruler of eighty-nine million people."

No matter how right Dwight was, the war opened opportunities for him and for his younger brother. In 1942, Dwight became the U.S. Army's chief of staff, General George C. Marshall's number-two man, and was soon dispatched to England to take command there, while Milton became number-two man in the Office of War Information, a position that made it possible for him to do his brother's image and reputation much good. Milton not only taught his brother about the importance of the press; he also supplied reporters with anecdotes about General Eisenhower and suggested stories and angles.

Good as Milton was, he could have done little without the active cooperation of the subject himself. Dwight enjoyed meeting with the press, liked reporters as individuals, knew some of them himself from his many parties at Milton's apartment and flattered them by paying attention to them. As Milton could testify, being General Eisenhower's press secretary was about as easy and rewarding a job for a public relations man as could be imagined.

Dwight's biggest problem came in early November 1942, when British and American forces under his command invaded North Africa and he appointed the French admiral Jean Darlan as governor of the French colony in Algeria. Darlan was known throughout Europe as a fascist who was collaborating with Hitler, and this appointment, although necessary, stank to heaven. In England as back in the States, there was a demand from liberals that Eisenhower be fired.

Milton Eisenhower, who by this time had been appointed by President Franklin Roosevelt as director of the program to handle the Japanese-Americans who had been forced to leave their homes in California and take up residence in concentration camps in the American desert, was none too popular himself. Nevertheless, he took up the task of defending his brother and flew to Washington to see Roosevelt, who gave him an audience to discuss the problem. Roosevelt asked Milton to draft a statement endorsing the Darlan deal. Milton did, but to his disgust Roosevelt changed the draft by using the word "temporary" to the point of redundancy and insisting that this piece of "military expediency" did not prejudge the eventual government of French North Africa. Milton changed some, not all, of the presidential statement back to its original.

Then he flew to North Africa, where he moved into reporters' headquarters. He flew into a rage when he found some radio commentators referring to his brother as a fascist.

Milton said that "unless drastic action were taken immediately," his brother's career might be irreparably damaged. "Heads must roll," he exclaimed. "Heads must roll!" Cuts in the broadcasters corps were made, and Dwight's career was saved.

For much of the remainder of the war, Milton stayed with Dwight, seeing to his reputation, which wasn't hard. By the end of the war, Milton was president at Kansas State College. By that time Tom Watson, founder and owner of IBM, and his friends in New York State wanted Dwight as the next president of the United States and thought the way to get him there was to make him president of Columbia University. In April 1946, Dwight, who was then still chief of staff of the U.S. Army, spoke at the Metropolitan Museum of Art. That night Watson asked if he would consider taking the job of president of Columbia. Dwight's instant reply was that Columbia had asked the wrong Eisenhower, that it should go after Milton, the experienced educator. No, Watson said, Columbia wanted the general. Dwight refused.

Thirteen months later Watson called on Dwight. "To my chagrin," Dwight wrote Milton, Watson again offered the Columbia position, urging "the importance of the public service I could perform in that spot and painting the rosiest possible picture of what I would be offered in the way of conveniences, expenses, remuneration and so on." Milton advised him to accept, which he finally did in 1948.

Then Watson and the others began pressing Dwight to run for the presidency of the United States in 1952. He was opposed because he had been a lifetime soldier, not a politician; Milton also opposed, as he didn't want his older brother to risk his reputation. But soon Milton came to so dislike Senator Robert A. Taft, the potential Republican nominee, and President Harry S. Truman, the probable Democratic nominee, that he began urging his brother to run on the grounds that if the choice before the American people was Truman or Taft, then "any personal sacrifice on the part of any honest American citizen is wholly justified."

Milton went on to lament that "sooner or later no matter how violently you may wish, on a purely personal basis, to remain aloof from partisan politics, you are going to have to decide what, if any, public responsibility you have. I hope you don't mind my saying that I am terribly sorry for you. I know you would like to keep out of all this. I know that instinctively you'd like to issue a blast and put a stop to it once and for all. But that deep-seated sense of duty which was drilled into you must be causing you to suffer much anguish."

Dwight finally, reluctantly, agreed. Milton would not campaign for him, but he did write speeches. In November 1952 the people elected him to be their leader. He chose his youngest brother to be his principal adviser. "The most influential person in the new government is not, officially, in the government at all," *Reader's Digest* reported in June 1953. "He is not and never has been in politics. He is Milton Eisenhower, Ike's younger brother." The brothers, the *Digest* wrote, "think alike and their thinking has led them to like conclusions and convictions." They had worked out their philosophy back in the thirties "in batting ideas back and forth." Ike especially relied on Milton for help in his dealings with the federal bureaucracy, because "few men know more than Milton Eisenhower knows about the vast mechanism of our federal government."

From beginning to end Eisenhower involved himself deeply in his brother's political life. It was inevitable that this would be so, given their intimate relationship. Indeed, Ike often said that had Milton not been his brother, he would have been offered an appointment as either secretary of agriculture or secretary of state.

Yet both brothers knew that in addition to avoiding the charge of nepotism, being outside the government allowed Milton to range more freely than otherwise would have been possible. He gave advice on everything. But despite his virtually unlimited access to the president, Milton insisted, more or less successfully, on remaining in the background. He made few enemies.

"When I say to you that Dwight and I discussed every major decision he made," Milton once told a friend, "I must be sure you have this in mind: Most persons in leadership authority like to think out loud with someone he deems to be intelligent, well informed, conscious of all the nuances from fiscal policy to political possibility, can be trusted absolutely never to divulge a secret, and whom he admires: it is that kind of person who should be the President's principal confidant."

At breakfast, over cocktails before dinner or late at night, the two Eisenhower brothers would discuss the problems of the world. The press, always fascinated by those who are close to the seat of power and have the president's ear, wrote extensively about Milton, but he insisted that he had no political ambitions of his own, never sought power for himself and insofar as possible kept in the background.

Had it been up to Milton, there would have been no Eisenhower candidacy at all in 1956. In 1955, Dwight had suffered a heart attack that left him on his back for a few weeks. When he finally recovered he convened a dozen of his closest associates for an intimate meeting in the White House. They all knew that the result would determine whether Ike would accept the Republican nomination for a second time. Milton intended to be an impartial moderator, but to his dismay not one person in the room voiced a single reason Ike should not run.

Finally, Ike asked Milton to summarize the discussion.

Speaking more as Ike's brother than as an adviser, and having already made known his own negative views of the Republican party and his brother's running once again, Milton took the opportunity to state what the others would not. He reminded everyone that the president was sixty-six years old and that, if elected, he would become the oldest man to serve in the White House. He had already had one near-fatal attack, and there was no guarantee that he could survive the campaign, let alone another full term. In Milton's eyes, the assemblage was urging his brother to risk not only his reputation but his life.

Dwight ran anyway. Over his second term, Milton continued to advise him. Ike himself summarized Milton's contribution best when in 1969, two days before his death, he motioned for Milton to lean close to him in his hospital bed. He whispered, "I want you to know how much you have always meant to me, how much I have valued your counsel." Of all the tributes Milton received, this was the one he treasured the most.

What Dwight had spoken to was the equality of respect and simple attachment between himself and Milton that had lasted for seventy years. Despite the public appearance of inequality in rank, power and achievement, they were always close to each other and maintained a relationship of mutual advice, giving and receiving respectful consultation. They had an utter trust in the other's esteem and love.

THREE

Brothers:
The Custer Boys

SOME AMERICAN BROTHERS continue their friendship and keep working together throughout their lives, as did Dwight and Milton Eisenhower. Many such relationships tend to break down into casual friendships after the boys leave home. A few stick together because the older brother demands worship and adulation, especially from his younger brothers. This was the case with George Armstrong Custer, born in December 1839, who graduated at the bottom of his 1861 class at West Point but who went on to great fame as a member of the Army of the Potomac, eventually becoming the youngest general, at age twenty-three, who ever served in the U.S. Army. As a student he was described by one of his neighbors as "Manly, exuberant, enthusiastic, with a noble, knightly countenance." By the time he was ten years old he had three younger brothers, Nevin, Thomas and Boston. By the time he was twenty-one years old he commanded a brigade in the Army of the Potomac, and at twenty-three it was a division of cavalry in the battle of Gettysburg. He was described in the *New*

York Herald as "the Boy General with his flowing yellow curls."

By 1864, Custer's younger brother Tom was old enough to enlist in the Ohio Volunteers as a private. Thanks to George's influence, Tom quickly received a commission and was transferred to Custer's outfit, the 5th Michigan, as a member of his older brother's staff. Nepotism was common in the Union Army; General Philip Sheridan's brother served on his staff, President Abraham Lincoln's son was on Ulysses Grant's staff, and so on. Tom did not have a cushy job. Although the two Custer officers tussled like the youths they were when they were alone, in public they maintained a stiff formality. As Tom put it, "If anyone thinks it is a soft thing to be a commanding officer's brother he misses his guess."

George Custer went to lengths to make sure that his staff was composed of hometown boys, which made it a happy, close-knit group. Lieutenant George Yates, from Monroe, Michigan, and a classmate of Custer, served as an aide. Another was Lieutenant Jacob Greene, and there were more. They all admired Custer enormously, although none quite so extravagantly as Chaplain Theodore Holmes, who told Custer in March 1865, "I cannot express my gratefulness to the Almighty that He should have made you such a General and such a man." Custer did something neither Grant nor William T. Sherman nor any other general dared to do—he brought his wife, the former Libbie Bacon of Monroe, into camp with him. In addition he had pets—dogs, goats, squirrels, a raccoon—with him. When Tom Custer joined the staff, Libbie wrote a friend, "He adds much to our family circle—for as such I consider the staff."

But Tom was there to fight, not do paperwork or socialize. Even though he idolized his older brother in all things, it was most especially in risk taking. Custer described Tom's heroism at one of the battles in the Appomattox campaign: "Tom led the assault upon the enemy's breastworks, mounted, was first to leap his horse over the works on top of the enemy while they were pouring a volley of musketry into our ranks. Tom seized the rebel colors and demanded their surrender. The colorbearer shot him through face and neck. . . . He retained the colors with one hand, while with the other he drew his revolver and shot the rebel dead. . . . With blood pouring from his wound he asked that someone might take the flag while he continued with the assaulting column." Custer had to put Tom under arrest in order to get him to go to the rear and see a surgeon. For his actions that day, Tom Custer received the Congressional Medal of Honor. Custer, who never got that reward, remarked that it was Tom, not he, who should be the commanding general.

After the war Custer was with the occupying force in Texas, and, of course, Tom stayed in the Army and on his brother's staff. Custer had many political problems, including what to do with and about the freed slaves and his own recruits. Tom helped. They went on late-afternoon hunting parties, or to dances, played practical jokes on each other and generally did their best to enjoy their situation. George Yates was with them, and, of course, Libbie. In 1866, George Custer was reduced from his wartime rank of brevet brigadier general to captain in the Army. He went to Washington, where he worked on Secretary of War Edwin Stanton to get a regular commission for Tom and George Yates, and his own rank moved up to colonel, all of which Stanton did. Custer took charge of the U.S. 7th Cavalry Regiment. Tom came with him, along with Yates and a bevy of men who had little or no use for their colonel.

The 7th Cavalry was in Kansas, Colorado and neighboring states to fight Indians and prepare the way for the coming of the railroad. Tom Custer was outstanding in his leadership, once detecting an Indian ambush and leading the forces that defeated the Indians, on occasion being given command of small groups of troopers to ride against the enemy. How tough this duty was in the dry, waterless, homeless desert can be best understood by considering the deserters—more than 10 percent of Custer's men took off rather than endure it. When three soldiers took off during breakfast, Custer turned to his brother and two other officers, whose horses were saddled, and called out loud enough for the men to hear, "I want you to get on your horses and go after those deserters and shoot them down." Tom and the others did, bringing back three wounded men, and Custer had no more problem with deserters on that expedition.

In 1873, Custer and the 7th were assigned to Fort Abraham Lincoln, across the Missouri River from Bismarck, North Dakota, not far from where Lewis and Clark spent the winter of 1804–5. He had Libbie, Tom, George Yates and some friends and other admirers with him. He bragged about the terrain and the game as much as Lewis and Clark had done, but he was there mainly to hunt Indians and clear the path for the Northern Pacific Railroad.

Custer had become one of the most famous men in America and many offers came in for his services. He turned them all down. More fame and more power were his goals, not money. The Redpath Agency, a New York firm, offered him a lecturing contract at $200 per night, five nights per week, for a guaranteed five months. This was as big as anyone of the day could bring in, about $3,000 per night in 1990 terms. He was in New York City when the offer was made and he turned it down. As he wrote to Tom that week, "I think the 7th Cavalry may have its greatest campaign ahead," and if he commanded it and defeated the Sioux, he might well become president of the United States.

Neither Tom nor any other of Custer's cronies tried to dissuade him. As the 7th Cavalry started out for the Sioux, after the ground had dried, Boston "Bos" Custer joined him, not as a member of the Army but as forage master for the regiment. Custer's nephew, Autie Reed, a teenager, was also there, to help drive the beef herd. As they set off together to find the Sioux village somewhere along the Little Big Horn River, they had a jolly time. They were marching through magnificent terrain and Custer was inspired by the scenery and the hunting. The only thing wrong was Libbie's absence, brought on by Army regulations.

Custer and Tom delighted in playing practical jokes at the expense of their younger brother. Once the three of them went for a ride away from the column and Bos fell behind. "Let's slip round the hill behind Bos," Custer suggested to Tom, "where he can't find us, and when he starts we'll fire in the air near him." They did. Bos came over the hill, looked puzzled, and Custer fired a bullet that whizzed over his brother's head. Bos turned and fled toward the column, Custer and Tom shooting over his head. "Tom and I mounted our horses and soon overhauled him," Custer wrote Libbie. "I don't know what we would do without 'Bos' to tease."

They slept in the open, around the campfire. "Tom pelted 'Bos' with sticks and clods of earth after we had retired," Custer wrote Libbie.

He would have been better off if he had spent his time worrying about the Sioux than teasing his youngest brother. On June 25, 1876, he found them. Although he had been told by his scouts that there were more Indians along the bank of the Little Big Horn than he had bullets, he ignored the advice and ordered an immediate charge.

Tom was with him, of course, and Boston was with the cattle herd. Seeing and sensing the movement of the troop with Custer down the ridge toward the encampment on the river, Bos deserted the herd and set out for attacking soldiers. Along the way he passed Private John Martini, who was riding with a handwritten message from Custer to Captain Frederick Benteen telling Benteen to come quick and be prepared for action.

"Where's the general?"* Boston asked. Martini pointed to the north and Boston put his spurs to his tired horse.

Eventually Custer saw his prey, who had in truth ambushed him along the banks of the river. Custer tried to charge and was repelled, forced to seek the high ground. There, surrounded by his gallant if foolish brothers and friends, he put up a superb battle. As one Sioux, Yellow Horse, said of him, "I never saw a man fight as Custer did." His brothers were beside him, just as brave, just as dead. After a few minutes, fifteen at most, Custer and his 225 soldiers were shot through, gone from the living. Where Custer lay, so did Tom, Boston and Autie Reed.   *No WAY!*

It was a brothers' friendship that had gone to the extreme, even beyond it. George Custer had the presidency to gain if he had won the battle, but Tom and Boston had nothing except credit for loyalty to their older brother, who had never done anything of note for them. Their worship of him, like that of many citizens of their nation, then and later, was based not so much on what he had done as on what he chose to represent and stand for. As he became famous, they had become known as the general's brother, which isn't much. Still, by sticking to Custer they had a chance, not

---

* Lieutenant Colonel Custer's regiment called him by his Civil War rank.

much of one to be sure, but still a chance, to be there for the ride. Now they were stretched beside him, not yet forty years old, never married, completely mutilated. They had given their life to their brother, their closest friend, now lying beside them.

FOUR

Friendship for Life: Crazy Horse and He Dog

CRAZY HORSE, BORN IN 1841, a year and a half after Custer, was the one who led the Sioux in their victorious battle with Custer. Even though he and Custer had much in common— a love for horses, for riding across an unfenced prairie, for the chase and hunting, for battle—they could never have been friends. Their cultures were too far apart, as were the things they revered and wanted.

Friendship among white Americans was generally asso- ciated with coming from the same family or going to school together, sometimes from working together, but among Plains Indians there was an extended family, no school and little of what whites would regard as work. Nevertheless, the Indians had deep, lifelong friendships, formed either when they were children and learned how to ride, make and shoot their bows and hunt or when they went on war parties to- gether, and once formed they generally lasted for a lifetime. So it was with Crazy Horse and his friends, most of all He Dog, a year or so older than he.

The two men were friends from childhood until Crazy Horse died. It was not because they shared characteristics. Crazy Horse was more a hunter and warrior than He Dog, who for his part was more an orator and politician. In his old age, He Dog said of Crazy Horse, "He never spoke in council and attended very few. There was no special reason for this, it was just his nature. He was a very quiet man except when there was fighting."

Crazy Horse was much more ambitious than He Dog. Rising to the top in the Sioux society depended not on social activities or speechmaking, but on battle. Chips, who was slightly older than Crazy Horse and He Dog, and went on to be a medicine man, later said, "When we were young all we thought about was going to war with some other nation [tribe]; all tried to get their name up highest, and whoever did so was the principal man in the nation; and Crazy Horse wanted to get in the highest station and rank."

Together, Crazy Horse and He Dog learned to ride, shoot and raid. Their favorite target was the Crows or other tribes, from whom they stole horses. That and counting coup—touching a live enemy and then riding or running away so fast that the enemy could not retaliate—were the favorite practices of the Sioux. Stealing horses was both a daredevil and an economic act; horses were the number-one possession of Plains Indians, essential to hunting and moving the village, always kept together in a herd at night and guarded by a teenager assigned to the task. He Dog was relatively indifferent at both challenges, while Crazy Horse was outstanding.

When they were in their early twenties, however, both young men were regarded as something special by the old men of the tribe. When they came back from a raid on the Crows, they were singled out for honors, especially the lances of the Crow Owners Society. The lances were three or four hundred years old. He Dog described the occasion: "Crazy Horse and I went together on a war trip to the other side of the mountain," the Bighorns. "When we came back the people came out of the camp to meet us and escorted us back and at a big ceremony presented us with two spears, the gift of the whole tribe, which was met together. These spears were given by the older generation to those in the younger generation who had best lived the life of a warrior."

In the 1860s, when whites began moving to the Plains, the Sioux began acquiring rifles and a rumor grew that the bravest of men fought without a rifle. Asked if it was true that Crazy Horse did so, He Dog as an old man denied it with a chuckle. He said that Crazy Horse "always stuck close to his bow or rifle. He always led his men himself when he went into battle, and kept well in front of them. He headed many charges." When in combat with whites, He Dog said, "All the times I was in fights with Crazy Horse, in critical moments of the fight Crazy Horse would always jump off his horse to fire. He is the only Indian I ever knew who did that often. He wanted to be sure that he hit what he aimed at. That is the kind of a fighter he was. He didn't like to start a battle unless he had it all planned out in his head and knew he was going to win. He always used judgment and played safe. Others were reckless."

The He Dog quotes come from Eleanor Hinman, who was a Nebraska schoolteacher three decades after the turn of the century and would drive her Model T Ford out to the Pine Ridge Reservation in South Dakota to interview old Indians. She had in mind doing a book about the Sioux and Crazy Horse in the mid-nineteenth century, but never got around to it. Her interviews, however, are priceless. (They are today in the Nebraska State Historical Society, Lincoln.)

Immediately following the Civil War, the whites built Fort Phil Kearny on the eastern side of the Bighorn Mountains, to provide a base for the soldiers protecting the Bozeman Trail, which ran from the North Platte River on to the gold mines in Montana. There the Sioux chief Red Cloud gathered an assemblage of Indians from various tribes and harassed the whites. His tactics tended to hamper but not drive out the white soldiers. So in December 1866 he decided to go after bigger game. The soldiers had to send out wood parties due to the cold. Red Cloud thought that if he could ambush the soldiers protecting the wood parties into a ravine surrounded by his warriors, he could kill them all. For decoys, he picked his best—two Arapahos, two Cheyennes and six Sioux, including American Horse, Young Man Afraid, He Dog and Crazy Horse.

When the wood party came out of the fort, a small group of Indians attacked them. The captain at the fort sent out a relief party of seventy-nine soldiers, under the command of Captain William Fetterman. When Fetterman emerged from the fort, Crazy Horse led the decoy party out of its hiding place, whooping and yelling, running in all directions, zigzagging, looking as if each man was terrified. Crazy Horse charged the soldiers alone, waving his blanket, giving the impression that he was covering a retreat of the remainder of the decoy party. Fetterman decided to give chase.

He Dog and the other decoys joined Crazy Horse, staying just out of effective range of the soldiers' rifles, luring them onward toward the valley where the bulk of Red Cloud's Indians waited, hidden by the ridge lines. When the soldiers were in the valley between the ridges, more than one thousand Indians gave the whoop and rode down on them. In less than a half hour, all of Fetterman's men were dead. Until the Little Big Horn ten years later, it was the greatest victory over white soldiers ever won by Plains Indians.

Through these and many other battles, some against other Indians, after the Civil War mostly against whites, He Dog was with Crazy Horse, sometimes beside him, usually behind him.

Until early 1869, when the first transcontinental railroad was completed, across Nebraska and southern Wyoming and through Utah, the buffalo were abundant and the

Indians did not have to exert themselves to gather in meat and robes. But the railroad brought the buffalo hunters and with them many soldiers, who could now move faster and farther than ever before, which cut down and soon all but eliminated the buffalo herd. After that the Indians had to subsist on deer and elk, which meant their men had to spend much more time hunting, usually alone. This meant that He Dog and Crazy Horse were not as bonded together as they had been.

From time to time they would go on war parties. In late autumn 1870, Crazy Horse gathered a group, including He Dog, for an expedition against the Shoshones. A drizzly rain started turning into snow. Crazy Horse muttered to He Dog, "I wonder if we can make it back to our camp. I doubt if our horses can stand a fight in this slush. They sink in over their ankles."

He Dog carried this word to Hump, another of Crazy Horse's friends and a co-leader of this party. "This is the second fight he has called off in this same place," Hump said disgustedly to He Dog. "This time there is going to be a fight." Hump rode over to Crazy Horse and said, "The last time you called off a fight here, when we got back to our camp they laughed at us. We have our good names to think about. If you don't care about it, you can go back. But I'm going to stay here and fight."

"All right, we fight," Crazy Horse replied. "But I think we're going to get a good licking. You have a good gun and I have a good gun, and so does He Dog, but look at our men! None of them have good guns. It's a bad place for a fight and a bad day for it, and the enemy are twelve to our one."

They fought all the same, but Crazy Horse was right, and soon enough the Shoshones had the Sioux on the run. According to He Dog, "it was a running fight, with more running than fighting." Eventually Hump's horse went down, and then Hump himself was killed.

The next summer Crazy Horse and He Dog worked up a big war party against the Crows. They rode at the head of the column, holding their lances high, full of pride in themselves and in the Sioux. When the time came, they led the assault, carrying their lances all through the fighting, always making sure that they were first and closest to the Crows, always last to retreat from Crow counterattacks. When the Crows broke off the engagement, most of the Sioux wanted to go home, but Crazy Horse and He Dog, plus Crazy Horse's brother Little Hawk, decided to follow the Crows for a while. The other warriors joined them, as they could not allow the lances to go unprotected in enemy country. The Sioux captured some horses and killed a few of the enemy, then broke off. When they got back to camp, there was a big victory dance. The designated artist painted the scene on the Sioux's winter-count pictographic history, done on a buffalo robe. The artist called it "When They Chased the Crows Back to Camp."

The next summer Crazy Horse ran off with the woman he loved, Black Buffalo Woman. Unfortunately for him, she was married to No Water. As He Dog related the incident to Eleanor Hinman, "Crazy Horse had been paying open attention to the woman for a long time and it didn't take No Water very long to guess where she had gone. He went after." He found Crazy Horse and his wife in a teepee on the Plains, burst in and shot Crazy Horse through the mouth and upper jaw. Black Buffalo Woman screamed and fled.

Here was trouble for the Sioux of the worst possible kind. Crazy Horse had broken the vows he had taken as a lance carrier, putting his own interests ahead of the well-being of the tribe. A blood feud might result. No Water's family sent ponies to Crazy Horse, whose family sent other gifts to No Water. The uncles of No Water worked for peace, as did He Dog. He arranged for Black Buffalo Woman to live with Bad Heart Bull in his tent, until Crazy Horse recovered. He Dog explained to Hinman, "If it had not been settled this way, there might have been a bad fight."

He Dog went on: "Because of all this, Crazy Horse could not be a lance carrier any longer. When we were made lance carriers we were bound by very strict rules as to what we should do and what not do, which were very hard for us to follow. I have never spoken to any but a few persons of what they made us promise then." After a pause He Dog expressed a bit of his anger: "I have always kept the oaths I made then, but Crazy Horse did not."

In the winter of 1875–76, much to Crazy Horse's dismay, He Dog and ten teepees of people who had thrown in with him decided to obey government urgings and go into the Red Cloud Agency, in northwestern Nebraska. He Dog was joining some forty teepees of Cheyennes, under Old Bear, who had agreed to do the same thing. He Dog explained to Crazy Horse that the women in his band were afraid, that his people had little children who could not run in the snow when the horse soldiers came. He Dog, who had been beside Crazy Horse in almost every battle of Crazy Horse's life, added that he had no need for any more coup or excitement of any kind. He did not need to prove his courage, but he did need to protect his helpless ones. Crazy Horse made no attempt to stop him, but he watched He Dog with a heavy heart, certain that his oldest friend was making a mistake.

But in March 1876 it was the Army that made a mistake. Because He Dog and Old Bear were on their way to the agency, they expected no trouble and had neglected to post scouts. The Army was able to achieve surprise in a dawn attack. He Dog and most of his people fled to safety, as did most of Old Bear's people. They escaped and fled to Crazy Horse's camp on the Little Big Horn. Thus they were there when Custer tried to attack, and a part of the Indian force that killed him and his men on the Little Big Horn. Later, many of the Indians accepted the inevitable and went into the Red Cloud Agency, but not He Dog or Crazy Horse.

Through the winter of 1876–77, the Sioux under the leadership of the two men moved into the Black Hills of South Dakota, which had been promised to them so long as the grass grew but was now under assault from white miners, who had heard about the gold in the hills. Crazy Horse often went out alone, to capture mules, horses and rations, and to kill the miners who were there contrary to government policy. But, of course, the government was determined to protect them, and various soldier parties were getting ready to do just that come spring.

He Dog strongly opposed Crazy Horse's long forays. "My friend," he admonished, "you are past the foolish years of the wild young warrior; you belong to the people now and must think of them, not give them such uneasiness."

In the spring of 1877, He Dog led his people into the agency. Crazy Horse stayed out. That May the Army sent patrols to find and capture him. Crazy Horse agreed to lead his band into the agency. Little Big Man rode on one side of him, He Dog on the other, his women and children and old men stretching out behind him in a column nearly two miles in length.

For a while the Crazy Horse band lived without incident on the agency, but on September 2 the Army ordered all Indians to move their camps to the base of the white butte, site of present-day Crawford, Nebraska, where it intended to hold a big council. Crazy Horse refused to go, telling his people he wanted nothing to do with the Army.

He Dog disagreed. He told his village, "All who love their wife and children, let them come across the creek with me to the agency. All who want their wife and children to be killed by the soldiers, let them stay where they are." Most began packing up.

Crazy Horse asked He Dog to come to his teepee; there Crazy Horse admitted that he was expecting trouble but he wouldn't go looking for it. He would stay where he was and hope to be left alone. He Dog asked, "Does this mean that you will be my enemy if I move across the creek?"

Crazy Horse laughed, then said, "I am no white man! They are the only people that make rules for other people, that say, 'If you stay on one side of this line it is peace, but if you go on the other side I will kill you all.' I don't hold with deadlines. There is plenty of room; camp where you please."

He Dog moved to the white butte. The Army leaders even gave him some presents to send to Crazy Horse. He Dog sent the goods by messenger, with a request that Crazy Horse change his mind. Again, Crazy Horse laughed in the messenger's face. Shortly thereafter, he tried to escape the agency, was caught and brought back. As he was being escorted into camp, He Dog rode up on his left side, shook hands and said, "Look out—watch your step—you are going into a dangerous place." But Crazy Horse failed to heed the advice. He was taken into the guardhouse and killed.

He Dog lived to be a very old man, highly respected by his people. He became the judge of the Court of Indian Offenses at Pine Ridge Reservation in South Dakota. In the early 1930s he was Eleanor Hinman's chief informant. She said of He Dog, "In spite of his ninety-two years and his infirmities, He Dog is possessed of a remarkable memory. He is the living depository of Sioux tribal history and old-time customs. Anyone digging very deeply into these subjects with the other old-timers is likely to be referred to him: 'He Dog will remember about that.' In interviewing He Dog one can hardly fail to be impressed with his strong historical sense and with the moderation and carefulness of his statements."

A pity that Crazy Horse was not so impressed by his friend's wisdom.

FIVE

Peers:
Eisenhower and Patton

EISENHOWER HAD NOT ONLY A NEED for friendship but a talent for it. He was a man to whom friendship meant everything. It sustained him and enabled him to be a great man. His gift for friendship made him capable of bearing George Patton's personality excesses and troublesome idiosyncrasies, and to value Patton for what he was—though not unconditionally or when Patton interfered in the Army's business.

The two men had little in common. Patton was a conceited, spoiled child from an extremely wealthy, snobbish family. He dressed as he pleased, said what he liked and did as he wished. He cursed like a trooper and told off his superiors with profane eloquence. Eisenhower came from a poor family in a tiny midwestern town. He had to support himself by working in the local creamery. He wanted to be well liked, and he obeyed his superiors. He did his duty quietly and efficiently.

Patton was an erratic genius capable of sustained action but not of systematic thought. Eisenhower had a steady, orderly mind. When he looked at a problem, he would take everything into account, weigh possible alternatives and deliberately decide on a course of action. Patton seldom arrived at a solution through an intellectual process; rather, he felt that this or that was what he should do, and he did it.

Patton strutted while Eisenhower walked. Both were trim, athletic, outdoor types; but Eisenhower was usually grinning, Patton frowning; Patton indulged his moods, while Eisenhower kept a grip on his temper.

Despite the differences, the two soldiers shared a friendship that survived two decades and (according to Eisenhower) "heated, sometimes almost screaming arguments. . . ." Their common West Point training—Patton graduated in 1909, Eisenhower in 1915—helped hold them together; however, other factors were more important. Both had a deep interest in tanks and armored warfare. Patton, five years Eisenhower's senior, had led tanks in battle during World War I; Eisenhower had trained tank crews in Pennsylvania. After 1918, when the War Department almost ignored the new weapon, Patton and Eisenhower, like those junior officers in England, France and Germany who believed that the tank would dominate the battlefield in the next war, naturally drew together. But beyond this mutual interest, they respected each other. Patton's dash, courage and recklessness complemented Eisenhower's stubborn, straightforward caution. Each admired the other and benefited from the relationship.

The two young majors met in 1919, and almost immediately they began an argument that would last until Patton's death. Patton thought the chief ingredient in modern warfare was inspired leadership on the battlefield. Eisenhower felt that leadership was just one factor. He believed that Patton was inclined to indulge his romantic nature, neglecting such matters as logistics, a proper worldwide strategy and getting along with allies.

A letter Patton wrote to Eisenhower in July 1926 illustrates the difference between the two men. Ike had just spent a year at the Command and General Staff School at Fort Leavenworth, Kansas. He had applied himself with almost monastic diligence to his studies and had graduated first in his class. Patton, fearful that his friend had concentrated too hard on such subjects as transportation, staff functioning and how to draft a memo, decided to set him straight. After congratulating Eisenhower on his achievement, Patton declared, "We talk a hell of a lot about tactics and stuff and we never get to brass tacks. Namely what is it that makes the poor S.O.B. who constitutes the casualty list fight." Leadership was Patton's answer. Officers had to get out and inspire the men, keep them moving. One or two superheroes would not do; Patton thought any such notion was "bull." Finally, he concisely summed up the difference between his and Eisenhower's approach to battle: "Victory in the next war will depend on EXECUTION not PLANS." By execution, Patton said, he meant keeping the infantry advancing under fire.

Eisenhower disagreed. Plans, he said, meant that food and ammunition and gasoline would continue to reach the men at the front lines, that pressure would be applied where it hurt the enemy the most, that supreme effort would not be wasted. The most difficult tasks in the next war, Eisenhower believed, would be raising, training, arming and transporting the men; getting them ashore in the right places; maintaining good liaison with allied forces. Execution would matter, of course, but it was only one part of the total picture.

During the thirties their Army assignments kept the two men apart, but they stayed in touch. It was a bad time for armor advocates: the Army had practically no tanks. Patton, disgusted, joined the cavalry, where he could at least play polo, while Eisenhower worked patiently through a series of staff jobs. Patton lived expensively—entertaining, racing around in sports cars, keeping his own string of polo ponies, and traveling by private yacht and private plane. This was in an army that was, for most practical purposes, poverty-stricken. During the Depression, Congress cut officers' salaries and introduced annoying economy measures on Army posts. Most career men tightened their belts, entertained frugally and associated only with their fellows. Patton's ostentatious display of his wealth was offensive to most of his colleagues, especially his superiors; they could not begin to compete with him.

Eisenhower, meanwhile, kept begging for assignments with the troops, but his superiors, most notably General Douglas MacArthur, liked to have the hard-working, efficient major around. Eisenhower lived according to the accepted pattern and was one of the best-liked officers in the Army. While Patton disported himself outside the system, Eisenhower worked from within. In 1940, for example, Patton—who had finally become a colonel in 1938—took command of a tank brigade of the 2nd Armored Division. He found that most of his tanks were not working because of a lack of spare parts. When a mechanic pointed out that many usable parts were available from Sears, Roebuck, Patton ordered them and paid out of his own pocket. He kept the bill a secret, but it probably ran into many thousands of dollars. As chief of staff of a division, Eisenhower often faced similar problems. His solution was to write a friend in the War Department and, with this extra prodding, get the materiel he needed through the proper channels.

When World War II began in Europe, Patton quickly forgot about polo and his active social life. Eisenhower was certain that Patton would go straight to the top when America got into the war, and in September 1940 he wrote his friend: "I suppose it's too much to hope that I could have a regiment in your division, because I'm still almost three years away from my colonelcy." Still, he thought he could do the job.

Patton might have had his doubts. In any case, he had a better idea about what Eisenhower could do for him. Apply for armor, Patton advised, and join up with me as my chief of staff. "He needs a brake to slow him down," General George C. Marshall once said of Patton, "because he is apt to coast at breakneck speed, propelled by his enthusiasm and exuberance." Patton himself understood this, and he thought Eisenhower would make the perfect brake.

They did not get together, however, until two years later. Eisenhower, by 1941, had become a temporary colonel and was chief of staff for the Third Army, while Patton had continued to move ahead in armor. He did so because of Marshall's willingness to overlook idiosyncrasy and to judge by performance. In 1940 he moved Patton up to temporary brigadier general and in April 1941 to major general.

When America entered the war Marshall called Eisenhower to Washington; three months later he sent Eisenhower to London to take command of the European theater of operations. In July 1942, Britain and America decided that their first joint offensive of the war would be an invasion of French North Africa and Eisenhower would be in command. He could choose his own commanders.

The first man he picked was Patton. He gave his old acquaintance the potentially toughest assignment, that of hitting the beach at Casablanca. Patton did it with success. In March 1943, following the battle of Kasserine Pass, Eisenhower brought Patton to Tunisia to take command of the U.S. troops. He told Patton to win a victory or two and take care of himself. Patton, Eisenhower stressed, did not have to prove that he was courageous.

Patton scored a tactical victory over the German commander, Erwin Rommel. A grateful Eisenhower gave Patton the most coveted combat position in the Army, command of the invasion of Sicily. Patton did well. His Seventh Army sent

the German and Italian opposition reeling across Sicily past
Palermo. On August 3, Patton visited an evacuation hospital
and talked to soldiers who had recently been wounded in action. The general went around the tent and chatted with a
number of bandaged men, asking them how they got hit. He
came to Private C. H. Kuhl, a young infantryman who was
sitting on a box and had no visible sign of wounds. To
Patton's query, the soldier said simply, "I guess I can't take it."

Patton's temper erupted. He lost control completely. He
said later that in his opinion most cases of "shell shock" or
"battle fatigue," which were common in all armies in World
War II, were just plain cowardice. He told Kuhl in a high, ex-
cited voice that he was a coward. He slapped Kuhl across the
face with his gloves and turned to the medical officer in
charge, shouting: "Don't admit this son of a bitch. I don't
want yellow-bellied bastards like him hiding their lousy cowardice around here, stinking up this place of honor!" He
stalked out.

Kuhl, it turned out, had chronic diarrhea, malaria and a
temperature of 102.2°F. Patton's slapping was not widely reported. Patton felt that he had done the right thing, and dictated a brief account of the episode for inclusion in his diary
and issued a memorandum to the officers of his command
directing that any soldiers pretending to be "nervously incapable of combat" should not be sent to hospitals but, if they
refused to fight, should be "tried by court-martial for cowardice in the face of the enemy."

Two weeks later Eisenhower got a garbled, incomplete
report of the Kuhl incident and another, similar one that had
taken place a week or so earlier. After reading them, he said
mildly, "I guess I'll have to give General Patton a jacking up."
He then praised Patton for the "swell job" he had done in
Sicily and ordered Brigadier General Frederick Blessé, his
surgeon general, to go to Sicily and conduct a full investiga-

tion, but he warned him to keep it quiet. "If this thing ever gets out," Eisenhower told Blessé, "they'll be howling for Patton's scalp, and that will be the end of Georgie's service in this war. I simply cannot let that happen. Patton is *indispensable* to the war effort."

In short, it wasn't so much friendship as it was a sense of *needing* Patton that kept Eisenhower from acting. Still, he wanted such grave and indefensible offenses stopped immediately. He wrote Patton, "I clearly understand that firm and drastic measures are at times necessary in order to secure desired objectives, but this does not excuse brutality, abuse of the sick, nor exhibition of uncontrollable temper in front of subordinates." Eisenhower said he did not intend to institute any formal investigation or put anything in Patton's official file; but he did warn that if the reports proved true he would have to "seriously question your good judgment and your self-discipline, which would raise serious doubts as to your future usefulness."

In conclusion, Eisenhower declared, "No letter that I have been called upon to write in my military career has caused me the mental anguish of this one, not only because of my long and deep personal friendship for you but because of my admiration for your military qualities. But I assure you that conduct such as described in the accompanying report will *not* be tolerated in this theater no matter who the offender may be."

Eisenhower then called the reporters in his theater into his office and frankly confessed that he was doing all he could to hold on to Patton. He asked them to keep the story quiet so that Patton could "be saved for the great battles facing us in Europe." The effort worked. The correspondents entered into a gentleman's agreement to sit on the story.

Patton, meanwhile, tried to make amends. He wrote Eisenhower, "I am at a loss to find the words with which to express my chagrin and grief at having given you, a man to whom I owe everything and for whom I would gladly lay down my life, cause for displeasure with me."

In the late fall of 1943, President Franklin Roosevelt gave General Eisenhower his appointment as Supreme Commander for Overlord, D-Day—the invasion of France. Eisenhower decided to bring Patton along. He told Marshall, who had doubts, that he thought Patton was cured of his temper tantrums, partly because of "his personal loyalty to you and to me," but mainly because "he is so avid for recognition as a great military commander that he will ruthlessly suppress any habit of his own that will tend to jeopardize it."

Eisenhower felt that whatever trouble Patton caused him in other ways, he was critical to victory. As he said, "The first thing that usually slows up operations is an element of caution, fatigue or doubt on the part of a higher commander." Patton was never affected by these shortcomings.

So Patton, who had been in the doghouse without a real command since Sicily, went to England to prepare for the great invasion. On April 25, 1944, he went to the opening of a Welcome Club that the people of Knutsford had organized for the American troops. About sixty people were there, sitting on hard-backed chairs in a cold, damp, depressing room, listening to dull speeches on Allied unity. When asked to speak, Patton ad-libbed that he thought Anglo-American unity was important "since it is the evident destiny of the British and Americans to rule the world, and the better we know each other the better job we will do."

Patton thought the meeting was private, but a reporter was present. Patton's remarks went out over the wire service and by the next day they were widely circulated in the United States, where he was denounced by both liberal and conservative congressmen. All agreed that generals ought to stay out of politics.

Patton, in short, had once again put his foot in his mouth. Eisenhower dictated a letter to him. "I have warned you time and again against your impulsiveness in action and speech and have flatly instructed you to say nothing that could possibly be misinterpreted." Then he sent General Marshall a cable expressing his disgust over the incident. He added, "I have grown so weary of the trouble he constantly causes you and the War Department, to say nothing of myself, that I am seriously contemplating the most drastic action," namely, sending Patton home.

Marshall told Eisenhower to do what he thought best, and on April 30, Eisenhower replied: "I will relieve him unless some new and unforeseen information should be developed in the case." Eisenhower felt Lieutenant General Courtney H. Hodges would be satisfactory as Patton's replacement—Hodges had no record of getting his superiors in trouble. Eisenhower admitted that he had about given up on his friend Patton: "After a year and a half of working with him it appears hopeless to expect that he will ever completely overcome his lifelong habit of posing and self-dramatization which causes him to break out in these extraordinary ways."

On May 1, Eisenhower met with Patton. An old hand at getting out of a fix, Patton told Eisenhower that he felt miserable but he would fight for his country if "they" would let him. Alternatively, he dramatically offered to resign his commission to save his old friend from embarrassment. He seemed on the verge of tears. The outpouring of emotion made Eisenhower slightly uncomfortable; he did not really want Patton begging. He ended the interview by dismissing Patton without having made a decision.

For the next two days Eisenhower mulled it over. He finally decided that Patton was too valuable to lose and sent a wire informing him that he would stay on. Patton celebrated with a drink, then sent a sentimental letter to Eisenhower expressing eternal loyalty and gratitude. To his diary, however, he confessed that his retention "is not the result of an accident," but rather "the work of God."

Eisenhower's aide, Navy captain Harry Butcher, noted in his diary that Patton "is a master of flattery and succeeds in turning any difference of views into a deferential acquiescence to the views of the Supreme Commander." But if Butcher saw something that Eisenhower missed, there was a reverse side to the coin. Patton bragged that he was tolerated as an erratic genius because he was considered indispensable, and he was right. The very qualities that made him a great actor also made him a great commander, and Eisenhower knew it. "You owe us some victories," Eisenhower wired Patton when the incident was closed. "Pay off and the world will deem me a wise man."

Patton paid off. On July 30, 1944, his Third Army began to tear across France. Later, his two great moments came during the Battle of the Bulge and when he crossed the Rhine River. "The present situation is to be regarded as one of opportunity for us and not of disaster," Eisenhower told his subordinates three days after the Bulge began. Patton grinned and declared, "Hell, let's have the guts to let the —— go all the way to Paris. Then we'll really cut 'em off and chew 'em up."

He had been preparing for his counteroffensive since the Germans began theirs, and was delighted when Eisenhower told him to stop his attack headed east and instead to direct his divisions north, hitting the Germans on their left flank. That was just what Patton wanted to do, and by December 26 he had battered his way through to Bastogne and stopped the German offensive.

In March 1945, Patton's Third Army reached the Rhine. A few American troops had already made a surprise crossing at Remagen, where they had found a bridge intact, but the main crossings were yet to come. British general Bernard Law Montgomery was to cross to the north with British and Canadian troops, but Patton beat him to the east bank.

Six weeks later the war was over. His friendship with Patton had made Eisenhower into the general who had won the war. Grateful as he was, Eisenhower continued to obey his superiors' orders, especially about getting rid of Nazis in the American zone of competition. Patton chafed. He talked about driving the Russians back to the Volga River. He got chummy with German generals. As military governor in Bavaria, he kept former Nazis and SS officials in the local administration because, he argued, no one else was available. His policy ran exactly counter to national policy, and Eisenhower ordered him to get rid of the Nazis. But except for a few prominent officials, Patton did nothing. He was sure that, before long, German and American generals would be fighting side by side against the Russians.

His area soon gained a dubious reputation, and the press waited for a chance to bait Patton into damning the denazification policy. It came on September 22, when he called a press conference and asserted that the military government "would get better results if it employed more former members of the Nazi party in administrative jobs." A reporter asked, "After all, General, didn't most ordinary Nazis join their party in about the same way that Americans become Republicans or Democrats?"

"Yes," Patton agreed. "That's about it."

The headlines the next day screamed that Patton had said the Nazis were just like Republicans and Democrats back home.

Eisenhower phoned Patton and told him to get over to

headquarters in Frankfurt right away. Patton arrived wearing a simple jacket and plain trousers rather than his fancy riding breeches, and he left behind the pearl-handled pistols he usually wore. The generals were together for two hours. When Patton walked out he was pale: Ike had taken the Third Army away from him.

Eisenhower gave Patton a meaningless paper army to command. Patton stayed in Germany, spending most of his time hunting. In December, on a hunting expedition, his neck was broken in an automobile accident. Eisenhower, who had returned to Washington to become chief of staff, wrote him on December 10. "You can imagine what a shock it was to me to hear of your serious accident," the letter began. "At first I heard it on the basis of rumor and simply did not believe it, thinking it only a story. . . . I immediately wired Frankfurt and learned to my great distress that it was true."

Eisenhower told Patton he had notified Mrs. Patton and had given orders that everything possible should be arranged, including the fastest transportation available to fly her to his bedside. "By coincidence, only the day before yesterday," Eisenhower continued, "I had directed that you be contacted to determine whether you wanted a particular job that appeared to be opening up here in the States. The real purpose of this note is simply to assure you that you will always have a job and not to worry about this accident closing out any of them for your selection."

Eisenhower confessed that "it is always difficult for me to express my true sentiment when I am deeply moved," but he wanted Patton to know "that you are never out of my thoughts and that my hopes and prayers are tied up in your speedy recovery. If anything at all occurs to you where I might be of some real help, don't hesitate a second to let an aide forward the message to me."

Mrs. Patton arrived at her husband's bedside the next day, and she read Eisenhower's letter to him. When she reached the end, he asked her to read the part about the job again.

Nine days later, George Patton died.

SIX

Nary a Friend:
Richard Nixon

LIKE EISENHOWER, Richard Nixon was a man of enormous talent and drive. Unlike Eisenhower, Nixon never developed a gift for making and keeping friends, which requires effort, hard work and talent. His relationship with his parents was good to excellent; with his brothers more or less satisfactory; with his wife acceptable although not close to a model; with his two daughters nearly perfect; with his political associates cold and aloof and, in the end, bad enough to do him in, not good enough to make him into a world figure like Eisenhower.

With Eisenhower, people always knew who he was. He played no roles, only himself. With Nixon, one never knew. His speechwriter Bill Safire said of Nixon that he "can don a personality by opening a door." With his secretary of the Treasury, George Shultz, Nixon could be the concerned leader striving for free markets and more personal liberty; with White House aide Len Garment, Nixon was a supporter of the arts; with HEW secretary Bob Finch he was a political analyst and older brother; with speechwriter Ray Price he played Woodrow Wilson, brooding over the fate of the nation; with associates Cap Weinberger or Herb Stein he was Herbert Hoover; with his congressional liaison Bryce Harlow he played Eisenhower; with Attorney General John Mitchell he was FDR, playing politics at the highest level; with White House aide Chuck Colson he was Harry Truman, socking it to the opposition. Safire concludes, "When he didn't want to be anybody but himself, he sent for Bebe Rebozo."

It is a mark of how many different Nixon personas there were that when the transcripts of the Nixon-Haldeman-Ehrlichman-Mitchell* conversations were made public, many men who had had intimate contact with Nixon over long periods of time—Safire, writer Steve Hess, Republican official Maurice Stans, Shultz, Harlow and others—were shocked. *They* had never heard Nixon talk like that.

How is it that Richard Nixon was a man without friends? How could a man who had so much talent, brains, ambition and success feel so insecure, snubbed, unrewarded, misunderstood and ignored? It is not insignificant that with all the words expended on him, Nixon himself has provided the most insightful analysis. He was reminiscing at San Clemente with aide Kenneth Clawson shortly after his resignation from the presidency.

"What starts the process, really," Nixon explained, "are the laughs and snubs and slights you get when you are a kid. Sometimes it's because you're poor or Irish or Jewish or ugly or simply that you are skinny. But if you are reasonably intelligent and if your anger is deep enough and strong enough, you learn that you can change those attitudes by excellence, personal gut performance, while those who have everything are sitting on their fat butts. . . . [When you get to the top] you find you can't stop playing the game the way you've always played it. . . . so you are lean and mean and resourceful and you continue to walk on the edge."

---

* Bob Haldeman was his chief of staff; John Ehrlichman handled domestic affairs; Mitchell was attorney general, later head of the Committee to Re-elect the President.

With Nixon, the anger ran so deep it never left him. He was the angriest American president. He was a man who could never trust others and had no real friends. Nearly everyone who worked closely with Nixon commented on this. Eisenhower told his secretary Ann Whitman after a meeting with Nixon that he couldn't understand how a man could go through life without friends.

Nixon had hundreds of associates, thousands of acquaintances. Most of these people admired him, and many of them appreciated the opportunities he had opened up for them. But unlike Ike, who was beloved by all who ever came into contact with him, only a handful liked Nixon. Bryce Harlow felt that "people didn't like him for the simple reason that he didn't like people." Secretary of State Henry Kissinger wrote that "Nixon had no truly close friends," and remarked on his "congenital inability ever to confide totally in anyone." Senator Barry Goldwater told Nixon in 1973, "No one I know feels close to you," and Goldwater knew every prominent Republican in the country.

Even with Rebozo and other supposedly close friends, there was distance. Nixon once said, "I never wanted to be buddy-buddy. Even with close friends. I don't believe in letting your hair down, confiding this and that and the other thing—saying, 'Gee, I couldn't sleep, because I was worrying about this or that and so forth and so on.'

"I believe you should keep your troubles to yourself. Some people are different. Some people think it's good therapy to sit with a close friend and, you know, just spill your guts."

Nixon thought of such people as weak. Others would regard them as normal and feel that it might be a terrible thing to go through life without at least one intimate friend. Not Nixon. Those who knew him said that sometime in his youth he must not have been loved nor trusted. Reporter Hugh Sidey recalled a remark Kissinger made to him: "Can you imagine what this man would have been had somebody loved him?"

"What do you mean?" Sidey asked.

"Had somebody in his life cared for him," Kissinger replied. "I don't think anybody ever did, not his parents, not his peers. He could have been a great, great man had somebody loved him."

The theme of the unloved boy is central to the numerous psychobiographies of Nixon. It was all his mother Hannah's fault, for spending too little time with Richard, too much time with his brothers or with herself. It was all his father Frank's fault, for spending too much time at work, too little with his son. Frank did not love Richard enough, so Richard could not love.

This author has many problems with that analysis. Who can say how much love is enough? Who can say that Nixon's childhood was in any way so exceptional that it scarred him for life? What son ever had a father who loved him enough? What successful man ever had a mother who was loving enough, forgiving enough, understanding enough? Frank Nixon spurred his son, disciplined him, made him work, demanded more of him. This helped make Richard ambitious, eager to show his parents what he could do; it is hard to see how it made him incapable of love. Besides, he loved Pat, Tricia and Julie, and they loved him.

"A man's character is his fate," according to the Greek philosopher Heraclitus. Nixon had gifts in abundance—brains, acceptably nice looks, good health, a marvelous memory, knowledge, superb acting ability and stage presence, a faithful family and awesome willpower, among others. Indeed, he had nearly every gift that the gods could bestow. The one that he most lacked was character. Virtue comes from character. That is why Nixon despised virtue and railed against it.

Another quality that he lacked was an ability to respect others. In 1986, Harlow spoke to the point, admitting that he could not explain it: "The President went through, and it is probably still in him, a process of some kind that made him disrespect people. I don't know whom he respects even now—really really respects."

Nixon put himself first, always. First, last and in between. In his poem *Chief Joseph of the Nez Perce,* Robert Penn Warren has Joseph wanting to continue the fight against the U.S. Cavalry, to preserve his own honor and self-respect. But Joseph asks himself, "What right had I/To die—to leave sick, old, young, women—merely to flatter/My heart's pride?" And then Joseph has a flash of insight. He decides to surrender, explaining, "A true chief no self has."

Richard Nixon was not a true chief. He could no more "no self have" than he could bring himself to love, trust and respect the American people.

He did have respect for many foreign leaders, above all, for De Gaulle, and also for Chou, Mao and Churchill in particular. De Gaulle was a model and inspiration for Nixon. The theme of coming back from adversity had an obvious appeal to Nixon, but there was more depth to it than that. Nixon writes about De Gaulle in *Leaders* with great affection, but also with insight.

"He acted a part," Nixon writes, "playing a role he himself created in a way that fit only one actor. Even more, he fashioned *himself* so that he could play it. He created De Gaulle, the public person, to play the role of De Gaulle, personification of France." Nixon quoted De Gaulle, approvingly, to the effect that "a leader must choose between prominence and happiness. A leader must endure strict self-discipline, constant risk taking, and perpetual inner struggle." Nixon allowed no one to get close to him, and shunned the friendship of his colleagues. Like De Gaulle, he "transferred away any aides who had worked for him for a long time in order to reduce the risk that they would become too familiar with him."

Nixon once told associate Bill Gulley, "The minute you start getting familiar with people, they start taking advantage." To begin to understand Nixon is to read his remarks about De Gaulle. How accurate Nixon was in portraying the deep and complex character of De Gaulle is a separate subject. But in describing his hero as a self-created man, a man of self-discipline, a risk taker, an aloof man who had no friends and who underwent perpetual inner struggle, Nixon was surely giving us an excellent self-portrait.

Nixon's private life, like his public life, was full of contradictions. He knew an enormous number of people at home and abroad, and was on good terms with most of them, excellent terms with many. He had friends in the political world, and among the rest, businessmen large and small, sports heroes, college presidents, all successful men. But of intimate friends he had almost none, except for businessmen Robert Abplanalp and Bebe Rebozo, and they were more often together for long periods of silence than for hours of conversation and sharing—completely unlike Ike and his friends. Eisenhower was only the most prominent man who knew Nixon well to comment on how odd it was that Nixon was so lonely in a profession filled with so many gregarious personalities.

Nixon himself spoke to this point. "The more you stay in this kind of job," he said in 1959, "the more you realize that a public figure, a major public figure, is a lonely man— the President very much more so, of course." His perception of Eisenhower could not have been wider of the mark; few public men have ever managed to be so unlonely as Ike. This was because he opened up with people and shared his feelings with them and enjoyed their company. None of this existed with Nixon, who pointed it out specifically to Stewart Alsop: "In my job you can't enjoy the luxury of intimate personal friendships. You can't confide absolutely in anyone. You can't talk too much about your personal plans, your personal feelings."

Nixon did not say why he felt that way; he avoided dealing with that difficult question by shrugging that this was the way it was for all politicians. But, of course, it was *not* that way for such men as Dwight Eisenhower, Lyndon Johnson, Jack Kennedy or Ronald Reagan, all of whom had a tight group of people they admired and trusted who were intimate friends, men with whom they could share something of themselves, indulge in prejudices and peeves, do some philosophizing about the nature of man and of the state, make jokes, relax, be themselves in a flow of rapport and exchange. Friendships free of cant, of rivalries, of double meanings, of manipulation, of suspicion, have been as precious as they were essential to many great men. But not for Nixon, who claimed to be trapped in a situation in which he could not be himself, not ever.

He disqualified himself for love by refusing to ever open himself to it and thus become vulnerable, except with his family, the one place where he did have an intimate relationship. That his daughters had quite stolen his heart there can be no doubt; nor can there be any doubt about the genuine pleasure he took from being their father, or in the love and adulation they had for him. The girls were happy to be with their father, and proud of him, and only wished they could have more of his time.

A pity that none of his fellow politicians felt that way about him. But when it came to an impeachment vote on him in the Senate, whether or not he had been guilty of high crimes and misdemeanors, nearly every single senator, in a body in which he had served for two years and over which he had presided for eight years, was ready to vote guilty. This was one of the prices he paid for being friendless.

SEVEN

A Lifetime of Friends

FRIENDSHIPS STRETCH across the horizon—fathers, of course, and sons, as well as wives, career acquaintances of every type, many more. The serendipitous ones come from college, either classmates or students. With them you attend the same classes, read the same books, more or less learn the same things. If you are a male you rush and later join the same fraternity, date the same girls from the same sorority, play on the same teams, all things that lead to a genuine connection. In order to enhance the opportunity for friendship, you must be open and able to reach out and accept an individual throughout your life.

This is true even though it is difficult to maintain a lifelong friendship in modern America. I had close friends in high school, but we went to different colleges, then off to different business or graduate schools, then different cities to make a career. We changed jobs often and lost contact. But despite these and other difficulties, I've managed to keep up with and stay close to a few of my college friends, among them Dick Lamm, Jim Wimmer and John Holcomb. In each relationship we had lost close contact during the decades we were making our careers and raising our kids. But around the time we reached fifty years of age we came back together, and it came as easy as slipping on an old pair of favorite shoes. These relationships provide a sense of continuity to my life, a reference point, based on shared memories and experiences along with a desire to do something of merit for our society.

I met Dick Lamm on my first weekend at the University of Wisconsin, in early September 1953, at a rush at the Chi Psi Fraternity Lodge (a rush is a social event at which freshmen look over the fraternity and the brothers—upperclassmen—look over the freshmen. In retrospect it seems barbaric but at the time it seemed important). I was seventeen years old, Dick had just turned eighteen, we were small-town midwestern kids, embarrassingly innocent and naive, full of good intentions and ambition for we knew not what.

After the rush parties, Dick and I went to The Pub, a beer hall on State Street. Neither of us had much experience with drinking—the Wisconsin age limit was then eighteen—but we got started learning how to do it that night, buying beer by the pitcher ($1 per pitcher, ten glasses to a pitcher), knocking it back chugalug style, talking nonstop.

We talked about books, the books teenage boys read in those days—Hemingway, Fitzgerald, Anderson, Faulkner, most of all Thomas Wolfe and *You Can't Go Home Again.* It was a unique experience for me, I had never before met anyone who read Wolfe.

Wolfe's title spoke to our situation, obviously, and as the beer did its work we grew increasingly maudlin and nostalgic over what we were leaving behind, then about how glad we were to be leaving the small towns behind, how eager we were to embrace whatever.

We received invitations to pledge Chi Psi and accepted. We got started on our educations. By 1956, at the beginning of our senior year, we had moved out of the Chi Psi Lodge and into a two-room apartment over The Pub. It was a year crowded with events and decisions—I got engaged, played football, wrote a senior honors thesis, got accepted into graduate school at Louisiana State University, where I would study under T. Harry Williams. Dick participated in a variety of activities, especially student politics, and got accepted to law school. But in my memory, despite all that near-frenetic activity, all we did that year was talk about books—novels and history books, books on politics and economics.

Following graduation we went our separate ways, as fiercely competitive, hard-driving young men, concentrating on getting ahead. We got our advanced degrees and started our careers. As I climbed the academic ladder, Dick moved to Denver and got into politics, beginning in the state legislature, then on to the governorship. He was twice reelected.

It is pretty nice having a dear friend living in the governor's mansion. I got in the practice of inviting myself and family to spend a night there when we were returning to New Orleans from our camping summers in Montana. We would pull into the driveway in our Chevy pickup, a couple of canoes on top, bulging with camping gear, a Labrador dog, nothing but tee shirts and cutoff blue jeans to wear. Dick and his wife, Dottie, made us feel as comfortable and welcome as if they were a regular couple in a regular home.

But of course it was special. I was writing political history in those years—the years of Vietnam and Watergate—so naturally Dick and I talked politics. We disagreed—he was pro war and I was anti—but our respect for each other grew rather than diminished. He was doing what I could only envy—participating in politics at a high level with great success. I was doing what he envied—writing books on politics.

What most impressed me about Dick was his integrity. I knew he wasn't making any money as governor, that the job was costing him money. Further, twelve years in the governor's mansion is all very nice, but in the process Dick and

Dottie owned no house and thus missed the biggest run-up in housing prices in history. They left the mansion with a 1970s-level pension, no down payment for a house, facing 1990s prices. I lived in Louisiana, where we took it for granted that a governor would get rich in office—but Dick didn't.

At the time he became governor, Dick resigned his tenured professorship at the University of Colorado. I was appalled and told him so. Surely the university would hold a position open for the governor. But he insisted. Later, after leaving the mansion, Dick refused to return to law school— obviously the university would have loved to have him back—or to practice law. Instead he took a post teaching public policy at the University of Denver. His reason: America has too many lawyers and he doesn't want to be a part of making more of them, or make his living by being one of them.

In the 1980s, I told Dick that if he ever decided to run for president I'd gladly take a year off and help in whatever way I could. In 1996 he finally did make a run, but without my help, as I thought he was not made to run as a candidate for Ross Perot's Reform party because Perot had stacked the deck and made it impossible for anyone but Perot to get the nomination. Instead I got involved in an effort to get General Colin Powell to become the Republican nominee. In the middle of that campaign, Dick and I went for a day-long hike in the mountains behind Denver. For me, it was a humbling learning experience. I had thought Dick was naive to get involved with Perot's party. He showed me how naive I was about national politics with a barrage of questions about phone banks, press contacts and handouts, fund-raising, target lists and strategy and the myriad of practical matters that never occur to an academic commentator on politics but which are meat and potatoes to the real politicians. In addition, General Powell declined to be a candidate.

Today our relationship is as it was in 1953, going places together—camping, canoeing, hiking—and talking about politics, literature, nonfiction books, life. As old men we are disgusted with the two-party system and made some feeble attempts in 1997 to get a genuine third party started. We have had a lot less success than Teddy Roosevelt did with the 1912 Progressive party, but the experience has reinforced our friendship, which is priceless. There was nobody I loved more than Dick when I was in college, and now that I'm a retired college teacher he remains at the top. We spend as much time together as we can.

JIM WIMMER and I were teammates on the Wisconsin football team. We were small-town boys—Jim from Wisconsin Dells, I from Whitewater—and had been big stars in high school. He was a center and linebacker; I was a guard and linebacker. One thing that brought us together was our hatred of the line coach, who was always yelling at us to run faster, hit harder, get up quicker, extend ourselves. The coach demanded that we give more of ourselves than we had in us to give. He seldom had a word of praise and when he did it was fleeting and grudging. He made us into better players than we ever thought possible and he bonded us.

He didn't have a lot to work with, which was another factor in our friendship. Most of our teammates were good enough to at least hope for a shot at the pros, but Jim and I knew from the start that Big Ten football was as far as our athletic abilities would take us. (I do have a boast that I was the last Big Ten player to play a sixty-minute game, against Ohio State in 1956—we lost, 21–14. The next year unlimited substitution came in and the era of offensive, defensive and special teams began.)

One shortcoming Jim and I shared was size—we weighed about 195 pounds each. Another was our speed. We ran the forty-yard dash in 5.3 seconds. Today these figures are laughable—in the mid-1950s they were about average. The biggest man I played against was Jim Parker of Ohio State (now in the Pro Football Hall of Fame), who weighed 250 pounds. Our fastest halfbacks and wide receivers ran a 4.7 or 4.8 forty. Today, the Wisconsin offensive line averages 310 pounds and these giants run the forty in 4.8.

Anyway, Jim Wimmer and I realized we were going to have to make our living with our brains, not our bodies, which was a painful realization because we loved playing the game, and would have liked to go on forever. Knowing that could not be, we hit the books as hard as we hit our opponents.

We were history majors and in heaven. The Wisconsin history department of that day considered itself to be the best in the country, which it was. As scholars, the professors were tops. As lecturers they were superstars. We had Chet Easum for World War II, William Hesseltine for the American Civil War, George Mosse for twentieth-century Europe, Howard Beale for American foreign policy, Merrill Jensen for the American Revolution and Merle Curti for American intellectual history. These men provided lifelong inspiration and insight for me, Jim and hundreds of others. It was a privilege to sit at their feet, and the best part is that we knew that.

After graduation, Jim and I went our separate ways. He got into politics, served as aide to Governor Gaylord Nelson, as state campaign manager for Hubert Humphrey in 1968, when he lost the presidency by a whisper, and finally as a lobbyist and consultant—by far the most successful in Madison. I went into teaching and writing.

We reestablished contact in the 1980s, when Jim asked me to be the speaker at a dinner at the Madison Club, an annual affair that he had created. Jim had maintained his love of history—indeed he was better read in modern history than many of my academic colleagues, had a better library than any of them and knew more than most of them. His heroes were Teddy Roosevelt and Winston Churchill. To celebrate Churchill's birthday in November, Jim created The Other Other Club in Madison. To explain, as a young man Churchill had been denied membership in London's The Club, so he had organized his own and called it The Other Club.

From the first, The Other Other Club was a sensation. It is black tie. It features bagpipers, champagne cocktails, a salute to the queen and to the president of the United States, an eight-course meal, with different wines for each course, with a pause in the middle for a frozen vodka, followed by brandy and cigars, and then the speech. It is given by a noted scholar—all the top Churchill scholars have been speakers—who is advised that in view of the hard-drinking audience, he should bring good anecdotes and forget the analysis.

Finally, each year Wimmer delivered the eulogy. The themes were liberty, freedom, sacrifice, defiance of totalitarians, whether Nazi or Communist—all taken from Churchill's speeches. It was riveting, no matter how many times you had heard it. More than anything else about the evening, it was the reason The Other Other Club was the most sought-after ticket in town.

Being with Jim anywhere was always great fun. His favorite TR quote was, "By Godfrey, this is fun!" I've heard him shout it out at hunting and fishing camps in Wisconsin, on the Missouri and Blackfoot Rivers in Montana, at Wisconsin football games, at our cabins at opposite ends of northern Wisconsin, elsewhere.

Jim lived big. He was a bold man and one of the most moral men I've ever known. His patriotism ran deep and wide. He loved Madison, even though it is the most self-centered, self-satisfied, politically correct, left-liberal city in

America, while Jim was the opposite in every way. He did more for the city, and for the university, than anyone else, contributing freely his money, his time, his energy and his genius for getting things done. When I started an effort to create a Hesseltine chair at the university in honor of my mentor, I turned to Jim to organize a matching fund campaign, which he did.

On a couple of occasions the Wimmer and Ambrose families have paddled the Missouri River together. One year Dayton Duncan, TV documentary producer Ken Burns's partner, joined us. Like Wimmer, Dayton had been a governor's aide (in New Hampshire). Dayton and Jim paddled together for four days and never stopped talking—mainly politics. Dayton later wrote the trip up in his book *Out West*.

In June 1998, Wimmer fell down a flight of stairs, cracked his skull and died. His funeral was one of the biggest in Madison's history. In November, at The Other Other Club, I was privileged to be able to say a few words about this great and good man, and to be present as Wimmer's son Jonathan succeeded his father as the giver of the eulogy.

Jim's death was way premature. It is something you get accustomed to, used to, resigned to, after you reach sixty years old. That is, by far, the worst thing that happens to you as you grow old—you start to bury your friends.

JOHN HOLCOMB was a member of Dick's and my pledge class at Chi Psi. We became friends around the activities of fraternity life, especially parties. We liked beer, we liked to sing when drunk, we liked girls and dancing, we liked card games, we liked each other. Often we studied together. We had a warm, affectionate relationship.

In the fraternities of the time, pledges became brothers by going through what was called hell week. This wasn't all that long after World War II and hell week consisted of a barracks room atmosphere, including a drill instructor. The upperclassmen yelled and screamed at us, kept us awake for almost a week, had us carry out silly tasks and do silly things, and if we refused beat us. It was really awful, with no redeeming feature, but everyone did it anyway.

As a Chi Psi in 1954 there was some physical abuse involved, primarily spanking pledges with a big wooden paddle, hard on our bare behinds. I can scarcely believe today that Dick, John, I and a dozen or so others allowed ourselves to be so degraded and humiliated, but we did. I knew John had back problems, and when they got him down on his hands and knees, I couldn't take it. I jumped in and grabbed the paddle. It took considerable shouting to convince them to lay off, but they finally did. Who knows if I saved John from serious injury, but he says I did.

After graduation, John went into the insurance business. We didn't see much of each other for the next quarter century, until a reunion at the Chi Psi Lodge, where John was at the piano, banging out songs, something he was very good at, especially after a few drinks. Over the years John had gotten pretty heavy into the booze. At one point his wife insisted on a divorce. More than twenty years ago he pulled himself together, remarried his former wife and hasn't had a drink in all that time.

In 1994, John organized a trip on the Missouri River, through the White Cliffs, a wild and beautiful section downstream from Fort Benton, for our Chi Psi class. About twenty fraternity brothers came along, with wives, children and a few grandchildren, over sixty in all. We had great weather. At night, sitting around the campfire, after reading the journals of Lewis and Clark, we would get to talking. We had known each other when we were students; for most of us, there had not been much contact for four decades. We slipped, fell, slid, skidded into the past, relating to each other, as we did when we were young, the same jokes and laughs, the same songs. Then we got to talking about our fathers, and in many cases about how they died, and about our grandchildren and about our wills and estates and philanthropic activities, but again and again we returned to our young years. So the conversation ranged over three generations, but was devoid of any talk about careers. Usually, in my experience, grown men like to talk about their professional lives, and how the stock market or their real estate is doing, but not once on this trip did that happen. The timelessness of the river—always there, always flowing, always has been, always will be—and the circumstance of a reunion with the friends of our youth led to talk about what has been and would be rather than what is. The guy who made that happen was John Holcomb.

When Moira and I got into a bad situation with the booze, we turned to John. He was a source of strength and inspiration. Without his encouragement and advice, his understanding and support, we couldn't have made it. Thanks to John we have things under control. Moira hasn't had a drink in three years, I for almost as long. What he did best was set us an example. As Moira puts it, being with John at so many different functions in so many different places over the years, and seeing him have fun without having to lean on a drink—he still plays the piano and sings and people can't get enough of it—has shown the way. What he has done for us and meant to us can never be measured, or repaid, but it is treasured, as is he.

I've TAUGHT lots of students over the past forty years, and stay in touch with quite a few, and am fairly close to a considerable number from various teaching posts—the University of New Orleans, Louisiana State University, Johns Hopkins, the Naval War College, the University of Wisconsin, the Army War College, Rutgers and some others. I'm not going to get into naming all my student friends—they know who they are. But there are four who are not only dear friends of mine but of everyone in my family.

At Kansas State University, I offered a seminar on American history. A dozen students showed up, including one long-haired young man who set out to shock me by using the F word and asking why was America in Vietnam, why was the country spreading fertilizers and weedkillers over its best land, why did the rich become richer and why were working-class blacks and whites fighting the war. His name was Dan Davis and he had been involved in antiwar movements that had led to his going to a mental hospital for nearly a year. His personality dominated the seminar. I agreed with some of what he said, argued with more of it and felt a chemistry between us from that first encounter that has not yet left us.

Within days I had invited Dan over to our house for dinner. For Moira and each of our five children, it was just as it had been for me—here was a guy who could make you laugh, force you to think and be thoughtful, tell a good story, get serious about politics, keep his dreams of making Kansas into the kind of place it might be, with family farms instead of corporate farms, cattle grazing on grass instead of fattening up on feedlots, good schools and roads and homes for everybody, and a sense of belonging. He could listen as well as talk, always taking your views seriously while forcing you to wonder how good they were. And that first reaction has just intensified over the past twenty-five years. We stay with Dan and his family on their farm when our trips take us through Kansas, or bring them along on a Lewis and Clark trip, or backpack and canoe together. All seven of the Ambroses turn to Dan when we have something that needs disclosing.

On his farm in Kansas he has cattle and vegetables, geese and chickens, goats and turkeys. He is as self-sufficient as it is possible to be in modern America. He has to work for wages—he is a foreman at a construction company—to make money to pay for things like a television, a computer, a pickup truck and the like, expenses eighteenth- and nineteenth-century farmers didn't have. But for the most part he is living Thomas Jefferson's dream as a small, independent farmer. He is a yeoman—independent, proud, productive. He is what the hippies in the 1960s dreamed of being, one of the very few who actually made it happen.

Dan introduced us to Ron Kroese, a graduate student in English literature, very much stifled by that process, married to Louise Quinn and living on a rented farm outside Manhattan, Kansas. They had a horse they rode bareback, and long flowing hair, and didn't eat meat, and embraced as much of a hippie lifestyle as was possible in central Kansas. They had most of the mannerisms and political arguments of the hippies, but what set them apart was a determination to learn how to farm without harming the soil.

We spent weekends with them on their farm. On one of those visits, in the spring of 1971, Ron and Louise changed our lives. The previous fall I had made myself unpopular with the administration of KSU and, not wanting to stay where I wasn't wanted, I accepted a position at the University of New Orleans starting in the fall of 1971. We went house-hunting in New Orleans, found what we wanted and signed a contract. We would take possession in early September. So we put the house we lived in in Kansas up for sale and in May a bid came, subject to immediate occupancy. We accepted it and thus found ourselves with five kids and no place to live for a bit more than three months. The only vehicle we had was a Volkswagen bus. We thought we would probably go to the family cabin in northern Wisconsin and live there through the summer. But Ron and Louise convinced us to do otherwise.

Go to the Black Hills of South Dakota, they said. Wonderful country, rich history, lovely cool, lots of campgrounds, a perfect summer. We were convinced. We had a month or so of camping in the Black Hills, then another month at the Pine Ridge Indian Reservation, near Wounded Knee. It was that experience that got me into writing Western history.

Ron and Louise came to our cabin in Wisconsin; we visited them in their home. We know their kids, they know ours. Ron is in soil conservation, organic farming, crop rotation and other ways to preserve the family farm. He has become an executive with a staff, office complex and not-for-profit corporation to lead. He has become a bureaucrat, but for exactly those ideals he held back in the early seventies, about conservation and the natural life and the good life.

In the fall of 1971 at UNO, I offered a seminar on North American Indians and this gawky youngster named Bob Stalder showed up. A week or so after classes began, we had a fire in our new home and had to live in a trailer in the driveway for a few weeks while the house was being repaired, new furniture and clothes purchased, and so on. It was hectic, obviously. Bob heard about our situation. He began coming over every afternoon and was a great help in the myriad of tasks that needed doing. He was also a fine student and exceptionally good writer. As winter slowly came to New Orleans, we started canoeing in the swamps with Bob. Camping and canoeing trips to the Ozarks followed in the spring. That summer, 1972, he joined us for an extended camping trip in Montana.

Like Dan, Bob has his own relationship with Moira and each of the kids. For my part, he was great to be with, cheery, bright, eager, an avid outdoorsman. We camped together for some years. He was my companion on a trip to Virginia to see Meriwether Lewis's birthplace in 1977; along the way we stopped at Lewis's grave in Tennessee and spent the night, sleeping in bags next to the gravesite. A Natchez Trace policeman came by and told us to move on; I pleaded, promised just one night, to clear out first thing in the morning, and he let us be.

Bob was with us for most of our early Lewis and Clark trips. He knows the trail intimately, having once spent a winter on the Lolo Trail; in a canoe he is my favorite bowman, and he tells good campfire stories. When we first were friends he was putting himself through college by writing sports for the *New Orleans Times-Picayune;* after he graduated he kept the job and was going places. Meanwhile I introduced him to Dan Davis and he fell into a romantic obsession with the idea of a family farm, so he chucked the sportswriter career and got himself a small farm in Kansas, where he lives today, with wife, kids and even a grandchild. He has to work in town as a carpenter to make it, but like Dan he is essentially a self-sufficient organic farmer and rancher, and wonderfully good at it and happy doing it.

We met John Homer Hoffman at Wounded Knee on the Sioux Reservation in South Dakota in the summer of 1971. He was there to be with Indians—not to study them, not to convert them, not to change them in any way, but just to be with them. He was a high school history teacher who had talked his principal back in Baltimore into letting him teach a Native American course. He is a great joker; he knows a lot of Indians; he goes west every summer to camp among them; he is an expert in running a rapids in a canoe. Our mutual interests first drew us together and we became regular fellow campers; over the decades since our first meeting we have spent some part of every summer camping with Homer, and often enough the whole summer. When I'm in Baltimore I drop by his school to talk to his class; when he came to New Orleans, I had him teach my Indian history seminar.

We introduced Homer to Ron Kroese and they have developed their own close friendship. They come to our Wisconsin cabin each year for a week or so of canoeing, drinking local beer, swimming and talking. I've written about a number of Indians. I always talk them over, as personalities, with Homer before I start writing.

All these guys, Davis, Stalder, Kroese and Hoffman, have our trust and love. They have added substantially to the joy of living. They have taught us, entertained us, led us, supported us, encouraged us.

I met these guys shortly after Johns Hopkins University and the Naval War College. They were not the type of student I was accustomed to. Their interests, their enthusiasms, their style, their thought process, were not mine. But their lust for living, their determination to draw from America its wonders and joys, caught me and my family. They turned us into people who could see and feel the country's glories even while being critical of its politics. They also gave us an attitude toward the Native Americans that reinforced and expanded my own. As for themselves, they were and continue to be people who found ways to live their idealism, keeping their essential being. We taught them how to read and love America's history, while they taught me that it was by no means dead and to live my life keeping to their ideals—organic gardening, for one, and raising chickens in a shack built out of recycled wood, and hunting and fishing on public lands, all while developing a coherent criticism of American politics that went beyond the Vietnam War to include the way the country was run to the benefit of its corporate citizens. And most of all, how to enjoy life.

EIGHT

Dearest Friend

As a GROWN MAN, my dearest and closest friend is my colleague for nearly three decades. Gordon "Nick" Mueller is some five years younger than I, a fellow historian and a man with whom I share vacations, politics, committee meetings at the University of New Orleans, sports and movies, and an endless stream of talk about politics, in and out of the university, also our parents and life in America. We give support to each other. He knows my wife and children, and I know his.

Like Ike, Nick has a talent for friendship. Nick was the man I had in mind as I wrote the last two paragraphs of my essay on Lewis and Clark, especially the part about how real friends have no secrets and tell each other no lies. We share all aspects of our lives—work, play, family. He knows everything about me as I do about him.

We met in the spring of 1971. Nick was a young member of the history department, just out of the University of North Carolina, a German scholar. He had a party for me in his French Quarter apartment and we had a strong sympathy for each other from the first moment. We shared sports, politics, history, any and all passions. We liked to party, to talk, to have new experiences. Our wives got on splendidly. It was because of Nick, more than any other factor, that I moved to the University of New Orleans, where I stayed from 1971 to my retirement in 1996.

Nick has taken me places and gotten me involved in activities I never would have seen or done otherwise. In 1972 he insisted that I go to Colorado and do some mountain camping and hiking. I had never before been in the mountains, but since then I've never missed spending at least some part of every summer in the Rockies or the Alps. For the first ten years of our friendship, we played pickup basketball two or three times a week. Nick insisted I get interested in sailing, which led to our purchase of a forty-foot boat and uncountable days and nights of sailing. Then he talked me and about four others into buying a small resort on Roatán Island off the coast of Honduras. We could make money, he said, and meanwhile have cheap but exotic vacations with our families. He convinced us; three years later we lost everything. But if the investment didn't pan out, it sure did provide some memorable vacations.

Nick's enthusiasm for Austria led to some of our best summers. He had spent his summers in the South Tyrol as a boy and studied in Germany as a college student—both his parents had been born in Germany and had emigrated to America. Nick wanted to give our UNO students—working-class kids we both appreciated and would do almost anything for—an opportunity to do what he had done, so he created the UNO–University of Innsbruck Summer School. Each year for the past twenty-five years he has filled the Innsbruck dorms with two hundred or more American students, most of them from UNO. He brings a dozen or more professors to teach, a wonderful perk for the UNO faculty.

Each year he brings a prominent person—George McGov-
ern has been there three or four times to teach about world
politics—and he has made UNO-Innsbruck the largest
American summer school in Europe, attracting students from
around the country.

After I became somewhat known in American academic circles I spent four summers in Innsbruck, lecturing as
Nick's prominent person. With Nick as our guide, Moira and
I have spent many weekends traveling and touring throughout central Europe. At least some of our children have been
with us on most of the trips: Grace stayed over one year to
attend the University of Innsbruck and earned a degree
there; Hugh stayed another time to attend the University of
Salzburg. These were years in which we had almost no extra
money, but in many ways they were the richest experiences
of our lives.

I no longer have to teach summer school to make a living and Moira and I have returned to Innsbruck on many
occasions for a weekend, a week or a month. We know the
mountains there, and many of the hiking trails, and a number
of people in Innsbruck, especially at the university.

We know the trails, the lodgings, the theaters, the
restaurants, and the location is superb for a trip to Vienna,
Berlin, Rome, Paris, wherever—but mostly we go because
of Nick. He knows almost everything about the city and its
surroundings, and there is nothing he likes better than to
pass on what he knows. I share the same strength, or passion, or weakness, or whatever, and I've showed Nick and
his family around Montana and northern Wisconsin and
the swamps of Louisiana and much else. Sharing your knowledge with someone who will appreciate it and take advantage of it is just about the best thing to come out of
friendship.

I loved driving in the South Tyrol with Nick while

he explained how Mussolini tried to make the province Italian rather than German after Woodrow Wilson gave Italy this part of Austria in 1919. When we visited a cemetery Nick would point to the gravestones where the German name had been obliterated and an Italian one put in. He would show us an elementary school in which German was forbidden, only Italian spoken. Or he would talk about the Romans and how they conquered the province, or show us Florence and explain its history. Or I would tell him about what happened here or there in World War II. When we traveled the Rockies, I would arrange to set up camp at this or that Lewis and Clark site, then read aloud from the entries in their journals. Wherever we were, the flow was always fascinating.

All throughout our careers at UNO, Nick and I spent the cocktail hour spinning fantasies. We taught at a brand-new city college, a school that was an unwanted stepchild of LSU, but we were committed to the city and the university. At first we were young and ambitious. I always figured I could write my way to the top of the history profession, whether I was at New Orleans or at Harvard, while Nick figured he could go to the top in administration. In our cocktail hours I would talk about whatever book I was working on and Nick would talk about conferences he wanted to organize, on leadership, technology, education. Or we would talk about new courses we wanted to teach, such as The History of the Last Five Years for our freshmen, about what went on in the world while they were in high school. Or we would talk about organizing a booster club for the UNO basketball team; or how to get a football team started at UNO, or costumes we could make for Mardi Gras, or buying a new sailboat, or new pets—usually dogs.

Whether it was a Honduran resort or starting a summer school somewhere else in Europe to complement Innsbruck, Nick would plan budgets, cash flow, marketing. I would express skepticism until midway through the second drink, when it became obvious to me that Nick could pull it off. I supported him, and damned if he hasn't made it happen.

I would fantasize about the books I wanted to write, on Eisenhower, Nixon, D-Day, the Battle of the Bulge, Lewis and Clark, Crazy Horse and Custer, a British airborne company in World War II or an American one that fought all the way to Germany. Nick is a perfect person to talk to. He is not only an academic entrepreneur, he is an excellent scholar, most especially of ancient history. He was always encouraging. Do Ike as a great and good man, he said, and he was right. Do Nixon as a mean SOB who nevertheless did much good along with all his manifold sins (think of Napoleon, not Hitler, he advised). Do D-Day as an epic (he got me to read Homer again, on the Trojan War, as preparation). Do Lewis and Clark as an odyssey (I reread *The Odyssey* before I began writing, and I spent a lot of time showing Nick around Lewis and Clark country). Do the airborne books as biographies of a company, he advised. I did.

For my part, I committed to helping Nick move up the academic ladder, which he has done. When his marriage was in trouble and it appeared possible that he might break it up, I stayed at his side, ready to support anything he might choose to do but insisting, as only the closest of friends can, that he needed to do a lot of thinking and pondering and considering what such a move would mean to Beth and their two sons and most of all to himself. He did, and he ended up sticking with Beth, which has been marvelous for the two of them and their sons—and, come to think of it, for me and Moira and all the Muellers' friends. If there is anything

I've given Nick over the past three decades, this is by far the best.

In 1986, I got the idea of establishing the Eisenhower Center at UNO, with the principal goals of organizing and hosting academic conferences on World War II and the Cold War, and collecting oral histories from the men of D-Day. By then Nick had gone into administration and was the vice chancellor for continuing education. He provided the umbrella for the center, found some office space, got me a secretary and student workers. Today the center, now directed by Doug Brinkley, is much bigger and a huge success.

In 1988, I told Nick I wanted to build the National D-Day Museum in New Orleans, on the site where Andrew Higgins designed and built the LCVP (landing craft vehicle, personnel—the landing craft). He liked the idea and got us going. He led me through the process of getting a federal grant, a state grant and private contributions. The project stretched out for years—we had originally hoped to open in 1994 on the fiftieth anniversary of D-Day. We have had scores of disappointments; we have made dozens of costly mistakes. But we have stayed with it, working together, never getting angry with each other. Today, Nick is the president of the National D-Day Foundation and we are set to open on June 6, 2000.

I love Nick and he loves me. He would die for me and I for him. We have no secrets. Next to my wife and children and grandchildren, he is the most important person in my life and the one who is dearest to me. Our trust in each other is complete. And we still have projects and fantasies that will go on for as long as we live. Our relationship has been a joy and a privilege, indeed an ecstasy. I can't imagine life without Nick.

This is what friendship could, should, might be. Growing together, supporting one another, keeping the other guy's dreams alive. It is not like the competition of youth. There is no element of struggle in it, no pushing, only lifting, drawing the other guy on, teaching, working in partnership without ever having to ask for help.

NINE

Faithful Friends: Lewis and Clark

Meriwether Lewis and William Clark became friends as adults, as Nick and I did. Unlike us they had dangerous adventures together, a partnership in which their lives depended on their trust and which produced astonishing results. Indeed theirs could be called the best-known and most productive friendship in American history. They put their lives into each other's hands. Lewis recognized that from the first, Clark soon after.

I envy them for their great friendship and adventure first of all, along with everything that went into it—discovering, almost daily, new plants and animals; making the first map of the western two-thirds of the North American continent. Lewis dined alone with President Thomas Jefferson in the President's House (today known as the White House), had Jefferson as his private tutor in such fields as zoology, botany, ethnography and astronomy. No one, not even Clark, can aspire to these experiences. No one other than Lewis and Clark can ever again be the first literate person to hear the western meadowlark sing, or to see the Great Falls of the Missouri River, or to step over the Continental Divide, or to travel on the Lolo Trail. But what I envy Lewis and Clark for the most is not the experiences I can never have, but their friendship with each other, an experience we can all of us hope to have in our own way in our own time.

Lewis and Clark have become so entwined by history that for many Americans the name is Lewisandclark. Although both men were born in Virginia (Clark in 1770, Lewis in 1774), Clark had moved to Kentucky as a boy. They met when they were young men, together in the Army for six months, with Captain Clark serving as Lieutenant Lewis's commanding officer. No anecdotes survive, or any correspondence between them in the next decade. But in their six months together they had taken each other's measure and started a friendship.

So when President Jefferson commissioned Captain Lewis to lead an expedition across the uncharted western two-thirds of the continent (to include the Louisiana Purchase—from the Mississippi to the Continental Divide on the Rocky Mountains, just purchased from Napoleon), Lewis thought first of Clark, by then retired from the Army. Lewis wrote his friend a letter in which he described the plan to get to and beyond the Rockies, then concluded with an invitation to greatness: "Thus my friend, you have a summary view of the plan, the means and the objects of this expedition. If therefore there is anything under those circumstances, in this enterprise, which would induce you to participate with me in it's fatiegues, it's dangers and it's honors, believe me there is no man on earth with whom I should feel equal pleasure in sharing them as with yourself."

Lewis went on to make a most extraordinary offer. If Clark could come, Lewis promised him a captain's commission and co-command of the expedition. Clark's commission would come along in due course. Lewis had talked to the president and obtained Jefferson's permission to add another officer. But Jefferson thought he had in mind a lieutenant as second-in-command, and certainly had not authorized Lewis to offer a captain's commission. Further, divided command is the bane of all military men. Lewis made the offer anyway.

Clark was more than delighted to receive Lewis's invitation. In his reply, he said he would "chearfully join" Lewis, and concluded, "This is an undertaking fraited with many difeculties, but My friend I do assure you that no man lives with whome I would perfur to undertake Such a Trip &c. as yourself." In a follow-up letter, Clark wrote, "My friend, I join you with hand & Heart."

On October 15, 1803, on the porch of General George Rogers Clark (he was William Clark's older brother) in Clarksville, Indiana, across the Ohio River from Louisville, Kentucky, Lewis and Clark joined hands and hearts. They talked through the evening. The next day they began selecting the thirty-man Corps of Discovery from hundreds of volunteers. They picked only expert woodsmen, unmarried, in perfect physical condition. Then they descended the Ohio River, went up the Mississippi to the mouth of Wood River, Illinois, across the river from the mouth of the Missouri, just upstream and east of St. Louis. Throughout this trip they shared the decision making—where to camp, whom to send out as hunters, what provisions to lay by, how and what to pack for a journey of they knew not how long through country that could not be imagined, what trade goods in what quantities for the Indians.

At Wood River, Clark was in charge as Lewis crossed to the west bank to buy provisions from the local merchants. Clark's commission from the War Department had arrived, six weeks after it had been sent. It was a lieutenant's, not a captain's, commission, Secretary of War Henry Dearborn explained, because there were no vacancies in the Army for a captain. Lewis was mortified; he had given his word. He might have said to Clark that he was sorry, but Clark, as an old Army hand, knew the ways of the War Department. So

Lewis would have to take sole command of the Corps of Discovery. Clark could come along as second-in-command.

But that thought never entered Lewis's mind. Instead, he figured his way out of the problem. He wrote Clark immediately, typically giving him the bad news first, then adding, "I think it will be best to let none of our party or any other persons know any thing about the grade." This was satisfactory to his friend Clark who like most Virginia gentlemen was rank-conscious, and it was done. Jefferson and the War Department thought of it as the Lewis Expedition, with Lieutenant Clark as second-in-command. But for the men of the expedition it was Captain Clark and Captain Lewis (which is what they called each other in conversation). They were co-commanders to their men, and what the men thought was what counted.

That, and their friendship. Their situation was indeed fraught with danger. They had ahead of them four thousand miles of wilderness, peopled by Indians who had to be regarded as potentially hostile until proven otherwise, Indians who had to regard all strangers as threats. They had mountains to cross, rapids to run, falls to portage. If at any time they disagreed over one of the daily, often life-threatening decisions they would have to make, Lewis could have pulled rank on Clark. But Lewis was confident that would never happen. So was Clark.

It never did. During the twenty-eight-month-long expedition, they had some disagreements: Lewis craved salt when it ran out and came to like dog meat, while Clark was indifferent about salt and could not reconcile himself to eating dog. That was about it. They never disagreed on a decision. They thought alike, thanks to their professionalism as Army officers and as explorers. They knew each other well enough to know how the other captain thought things through. When they had to make a decision on their own, because the other captain was away on a side exploration, they did so with the confidence that had consultation been possible the decision would have been the same.

They were superb company commanders. They knew how to push the men to but not past the breaking point, how to get more out of the men than the men ever realized they had it in themselves to give. And out of themselves. No matter how cold they were, how exhausted, how dangerous their situation, how miserable their existence, or how hungry and worried and frightened, they never spoke sharply to one another.

They nursed each other. Lewis pulled thorns from Clark's feet and bathed them. Clark ministered to Lewis. On the return journey, Lewis got shot in the ass in a hunting accident, a wound so painful he had to lie on his belly in the canoe for the next month. Clark washed the wound twice a day for those weeks, and packed it with lint, to ensure healing from the inside out. Finally he was able to write in his journal, "I am happy to have it in my power to Say that my worthy friend Capt Lewis is recovering fast, he walked a little to day for the first time."

When they got to St. Louis, in September 1806, Lewis's first act was to write Jefferson to set him straight on this business of Clark's commission. "With rispect to the exertions and services rendereed by that esteemable man Capt. William Clark in the course of our voyage I cannot say too much; if sir any credit be due for the success of the arduous enterprise in which we have been mutually engaged, he is equally with myself entitled to your consideration and that of our common country." Over the next year Lewis worked on the president and the Congress to make certain that Clark was treated equally with himself when it came to handing out rewards and honors. And it was Lewis who first referred to the voyage as the Lewis and Clark Expedition.

Shortly after their return, Clark married his niece Julia Hancock. Jefferson appointed Clark to a generalship and to command of the Indian territory in Louisiana, with headquarters in St. Louis. Jefferson had already made Lewis the governor of Upper Louisiana, again with headquarters in St. Louis, so Lewis was there when the Clarks arrived. Lewis gave Mrs. Julia Clark a gift he had ordered from New Orleans, a complete set of Shakespeare. For some months the three of them lived in a house Lewis had picked out, but Julia was pregnant and as her time approached she kicked Lewis out of the house. He continued to share his office with Clark and took his meals with him and Julia. When the baby was born, it was a boy. Clark named his first child Meriwether Lewis Clark.

Lewis's heartbreaking financial and mental decline in 1808 and 1809 distressed Clark greatly. He loaned Lewis money, kept him out of scenes at taverns and balls, looked after him as best he could. But Lewis's troubles ran very deep—depression, daily doses of opium (which he took for his malaria), whisky, unsuccessful land speculation, rejection in love—and they all just got worse. The government, now headed by President James Madison, demanded that he pay up on some chits he had signed, for trade goods for the Indians. Having no money, he set off for Washington to straighten things out. The day after his departure, Clark wrote one of his brothers that Lewis "is ruined. . . . I have not Spent Such a day as yesterday for maney years. . . . his Crediters all flocking in . . . distressed him much, which he expressed to me in Such terms as to Cause a Cempothy which is not yet off—I do not beleve there was ever an honester man in Louisiana nor one who had pureor motives than Govr. Lewis. if his mind had been at ease I Should have parted Cherefully."

The two men never saw each other again. But on the

last day of his life, Lewis took a seat on the porch of Mrs. Grinder's cabin on the Natchez Trace and looked west, down the Natchez Trail, as the sun began to set. He watched the sun go down and the light began to fade and he said to his servant that "General Clark had heard of his difficulty and was coming on. He would set things straight. He always did." Clark had saved him at uncountable rapids, in the Rocky Mountains, from wolves and charging buffalo, during flash floods and hailstorms, on innumerable occasions. Lewis watched for him until it was dark.

But, of course, Clark was in St. Louis, not having heard that Lewis had twice tried to kill himself on the boat trip from St. Louis to Memphis, that he had tried again while under observation in Memphis, and that it was feared he would try one more time on his trip to Washington. Clark was not coming on. He had saved Lewis on many occasions, but he could not save his friend and partner when Lewis was determined to kill himself.

What Clark was doing was thinking about what he and Lewis had accomplished. Mapping the Missouri and Columbia Rivers, and the Lolo Trail over the Bitterroot Mountains. Describing Indian tribes never before seen by white men, including the Shoshones and Nez Perce. Discovering and preserving all those plants and animals. And more.

What Lewis and Clark had done, first of all, was to demonstrate that there is nothing that men cannot do if they get themselves together and act as a team. Here you had thirty-two men who had become so close, so bonded, that when they heard a cough at night they knew instantly who had a cold. They could see a man's silhouette in the dark and know who it was. They knew who liked salt on his meat and who was indifferent. They knew who was the best shot, the fastest runner, the one who could get a fire going the quickest on a rainy morning. They had become a band of brothers, and together they were able to accomplish feats that we just stand astonished at today.

It was the captains who welded the Corps of Discovery into a team—indeed, into a family. This was their greatest accomplishment. It was based on their professionalism, of course, but also on their friendship. It was the most famous friendship in American history, based first of all on their common birth and later attraction, partly on their personalities, mainly on the dangerous and arduous task they set out to do together, coupled with their certain knowledge that if they disagreed with each other, shouted or yelled, tried to set one of the men of the Corps of Discovery against any one or all of the others, then there was no way they could make it to the Pacific Ocean and back. Their journals, America's epic poem, cover everything. They contain not one hint that in their twenty-eight-month expedition the captains exchanged even one sharp word.

Friendship is different from all other relationships. Unlike acquaintanceship it is based on love. Unlike lovers and married couples it is free of jealousy. Unlike children and parents it knows neither criticism nor resentment. Friendship has no status in law. Business partnerships are based on a contract. So is marriage. Parents are bound by the law, as are children. But friendship is freely entered into, freely given, freely exercised.

Friends never cheat each other, or take advantage, or lie. Friends do not spy on one another, yet they have no secrets. Friends glory in each other's successes and are downcast by the failures. Friends minister to each other, nurse each other. Friends give to each other, worry about each other, stand always ready to help. Perfect friendship is rarely achieved, but at its height it is an ecstasy. For Lewis and Clark, it was such an ecstasy, and the critical factor in their great success. But even at its highest, friendship is human, not godlike. For all his efforts and intentions, Clark could not save Lewis. But they gave to each other everything that can be drawn from a friendship, including their finest moments. Through their trust of each other they put themselves into the top rank of world explorers. And they gave to their country its epic poem while introducing the American people to the American West.

TEN

Combat Friends: The Men of Easy Company

THERE IS A FORM OF FRIENDSHIP that I've never experienced, though I have spent a lot of time wondering about it and talking and writing about it. The coaches told us during football practice in college that what we were doing was as close as young men could come to being in combat. We believed it at the time; today I know how utterly false that is. It is not like combat. Nothing is. Combat requires all the nerves, all the physical attributes, every bit of the training. It is only in combat, nowhere else, where time is measured in other ways than by clocks or calendars. Only in combat does the soldier realize that he is in the worst situation that can ever be imagined, that nothing else can compare to it, that the longer he stays where he is the more likely that he will be dead, or if he is extremely lucky he will be wounded. Only in combat is one in a position in which youngsters his age he doesn't know, has never met, are trying to kill him—and he is trying to kill them.

I wrote an account of the men of Easy Company, 506th

Parachute Infantry Regiment (PIR), 101st Airborne, from their banding together in 1942 on through to their being discharged from the Army in 1945. These were the best men I've ever known. I visited one of them at his home beside a North Carolina golf course, and there I met a buddy of his from Philadelphia. I visited another at his magnificent house outside Hershey, Pennsylvania, where he had invited other enlisted men to come talk to me. I spent a week at another house on the Oregon coast. I met a lumberjack from Oregon and a fisherman from Alaska and a schoolteacher from the state of Washington. I was a boy in 1942 when these guys were thrown together and I thought then and ever since that these volunteers for the airborne were what combat soldiers should be. I still think so.

I told the story of their training, their shipment to a small town in England, their preparation for combat, the loss of their captain just before D-Day, the experiences they had on D-Day and in the combat over the next month or so, their dropping into Holland in September and their combat there, the tough time they had in Bastogne and their experience in the months from the Battle of the Bulge to the German surrender. It was a great story and a terribly sad one, so many lost in the fighting, and an inspiring one, as they did their part to make sure it was the United States that won the war. I'm not going to tell any of those stories here; instead I'm going to concentrate on the friendships they formed and how they worked out.

In Holland, Lieutenant Richard Winters of Easy Company was put into the position of executive officer for the 2nd Battalion of the 506th PIR, which put him into daily contact with Lieutenant Louis Nixon, who was Battalion S-3, or intelligence officer.

They hardly could have been more different. Winters grew up in a middle-class home; Nixon's father was fabulously wealthy. Winters had not gotten out of Pennsylvania in his teenage years; Nixon had lived in various parts of Europe. Winters was a graduate of a small college; Nixon came from Yale. Winters never swore or drank; Nixon was an alcoholic. But they were the closest of friends because what they had in common was a dedication to the job at hand and a remarkable ability to do that job. Every member of Easy told me that Winters was the best combat commander he ever saw, while Nixon was the most brilliant staff officer he knew in the war.

"Nixon was a hard man to get out of the sack in the morning," according to Winters. One day in November 1944, Winters wanted to get an early start. Nixon, as usual, could not be talked into getting up. Winters went to his bed, grabbed his feet while he was still in his sleeping bag and threw them over his shoulder.

"Are you going to get up?"

"Go away, leave me alone."

Winters noticed that the water pitcher was half full. Still holding Nixon's feet on his shoulder, he grabbed the pitcher and started pouring the contents on Nixon's face. Nixon opened his eyes. He was horrified. "No! No!" he begged. Too late, the contents were on their way. Only then did Winters realize that Nixon had not gone outside to piss away the liquor he had drunk, but used the water pitcher instead.

Nixon yelled and swore, then started laughing. The two officers decided to go into Nijmegen to investigate the rumor that hot showers were available for officers there.

A couple of months later, in the Bulge, Easy's losses were heavy. Exact figures are impossible to come by; in the hurry-up movement out of their base camp in Mourmelon, France, the company roster was not completed; replacements for Bastogne came in as individuals and so were not properly accounted for on the rolls; wounded men dropped out of the line only to come back a few days later. An estimate is that

Easy went into Belgium with 121 officers and men, received about two dozen replacements, or a total of 148, and came out with 63, meaning 85 either killed in action or wounded badly enough to be pulled out of line.

The best description of the cost of the Battle of the Bulge to Easy Company comes from Private Ken Webster, who rejoined the company during the truck ride from Belgium to Alsace. Webster had been wounded in the leg in October in Holland; now it was mid-January. He wrote in his diary, "When I saw what remained of the 1st platoon, I could have cried; eleven men were left out of forty. Nine of them were old soldiers who had jumped in either Holland or Normandy or both: McCreary, Liebgott, Marsh, Cobb, Wiseman, Lyall, Martin, Rader, and Sholty." Looking at the unwounded in the truck, Webster went on, "I'm not sure that anybody who lived through the Bulge hasn't carried with him, in some hidden ways, the scars. Perhaps that is the factor that helps keep Easy men bonded so unusually close together."

They knew each other at a level only those who have fought together in a variety of tactical situations can achieve, as only those who endured together the extreme suffering of combined cold, not enough food and little sleep while living in constant tension could attain.

They knew each fear together. Not only the fear of death or wound, but the fear that all this was for nothing. One of their buddies wrote, "The deepest fear of my war years, one still with me, is that these happenings had no real purpose. How often I wrote in my war journals that unless that day had some positive significance for my future life, it could not possibly be worth the pain it cost."

They got through the Bulge because the company had become a family. They had held together at the critical moments; in the snow outside the village of Foy because First

Sergeant Carwood Lipton and his fellow NCOs provided leadership, continuity and cohesiveness. Despite a new commanding officer and new platoon lieutenants and enlisted recruits, the spirit of Easy Company was alive, thanks to the sergeants. Having Winters as 2nd Battalion executive officer was a great help. And Captain Ronald Speirs was proving to be an excellent company commander, able to draw out of the company its best. But most of all it was the sense of being a family that kept the men together.

That spirit was well described by Webster. Although wounded twice, he would not allow his parents to use their considerable influence to get him out of the front lines and back in the States. He would not accept any position of responsibility within E Company. He was a Harvard intellectual who had made his decision on what his point of view to World War II would be and stuck to it.

He was a man of books and libraries, a reader and a writer, sensitive, level headed, keenly observant, thoughtful, well educated. Here he was thrown in the most intimate contact with ill-educated hillbillies, southern farmers, coal miners, lumbermen, fishermen and so on. Of the enlisted men in Easy Company who had been to college, most were business or education majors. Webster was thrown in with a group of men with whom he had nothing in common. He would not have particularly liked or disliked them in civilian life, he just would not have known them.

Yet it was among this unlikely group of men that Webster found his closest friendships and enjoyed most thoroughly the sense of identification with others.

"It was good to be back with fellows I knew and could trust," he wrote. "Listening to the chatter in the truck, I felt warm and relaxed inside, like a lost child who has returned to a bright home full of love after wandering in a cold black forest."

Private Kurt Vonnegut had been in the Army's special training program, a student at Cornell University, very bright and sophisticated. He was pulled out and put into the 106th Division and hurried off to the Battle of the Bulge. There he linked up with working-class kids of all types in a rifle squad. He later said, "Those guys were the best guys I ever met." That is the way it is with someone who has saved your life, and you have saved him.

Almost wherever they were, the men of Easy Company—like all infantrymen of the U.S. Army—spent their time in foxholes. There they talked, softly, to relieve the boredom or the tension. Sergeant Robert Rader and Private Don Hoobler of Easy Company came from the same town on the banks of the Ohio River. "Don and I would talk all night about home, our families, people and places, and what the hell we were doing in a predicament like this," Rader said. Private Ralph Spina recalled discussing with his foxhole mate "politics, the world's problems, plus our own. Wishing we had a drink or a hot meal, preferably in that order. We talked about what we were going to do when we got home, about a trip to Paris, go to the Folies. Mainly we talked about going home."

Sergeant Clarence Lyall stayed in the Army and made a career out of the paratroopers. He made two combat jumps in Korea and in 1954 was assigned to the 29th French Parachute Regiment as an adviser. The 29th was at Dien Bien Phu. Lyall got out two weeks before the garrison surrendered. He is one of a small number who have made four combat jumps.

Sergeant Robert "Burr" Smith stayed in the paratroopers, where he got a commission and eventually became a lieutenant colonel. He commanded a Special Forces Reserve unit in San Francisco. In December 1979 he wrote to Winters.

Eventually my reserve assignment led me to a new career with a government agency, which in turn led to eight years in Laos as a civilian advisor to a large irregular force. I continued to jump regularly until 1974, when lack of interest drove me to hang gliding, and that has been my consuming passion ever since. . . . For the present I am assigned as a special assistant to the Commander of Delta Force, the counter-terror task force at Fort Bragg. My specialties are (surprise! surprise!): airborne operations, light weapons, and small unit operations.

My office is on Buckner Road, right across the street from where we were just before leaving for England. The old buildings are exactly as you last saw them and are still in daily use. . . .

Funny thing about "The Modern Army," Dick. I am assigned to what is reputed to be the best unit in the U.S. Army, the Delta Force, and I believe that it is. Still, on a man-for-man basis, I'd choose my wartime paratroop company *any time!* We had something there for three years that will never be equalled.

He was scheduled to go on the mission to Iran to rescue the hostages in 1980, but when the CIA learned this, it forbade him to go because he knew so many secrets. "So I missed what certainly would have been the last adventure in my life," he wrote Winters. "I had lived, worked and trained with Delta every day for nearly two years, Dick, and I *Hated* to be left behind."

That got Smith going on leadership. He wrote of Winters: "You were blessed (some would say rewarded) with the utter respect and admiration of 120 soldiers, essentially civilians in uniform, who would have followed you to certain death. I've been a soldier most of my adult life. In that time I've met only a handful of great soldiers, and of that handful only half or less come from my WWII experience, and two of them came from ol' Easy—you and Bill Guarnere. The rest of us were O.K. . . . good soldiers by-and-large, and a few were better than average, but I know as much about 'Grace Under Pressure' as most men, and a lot more about it than some. You had it."

In 1980, riding an experimental hang glider, Smith crashed and suffered severe injuries. In operating on his lungs, the doctors discovered a cancer. Rader, who had pulled Smith out of a flooded field on June 6, 1944, visited him in the hospital. They played a name game—one would call out the name of a Toccoa man (Toccoa was their camp as recruits), the other would supply a brief word portrait. Shortly thereafter, Smith died.

Sergeant Mike Ranney took a journalism degree at the University of North Dakota, then had a successful career as a reporter, newspaper editor and public relations consultant. He and his wife, Julia, had five daughters, seven grandsons. In 1980 he began publishing what he called "The Spasmodic Newsletter of Easy Company." Some samples:

1980: "The reunion this summer in Nashville is shaping up as one of the great turnouts in E Company history. A partial list of the attendees—Dick Winters, Harry Welsh, Moose Heyliger and Buck Compton from the officers; Chuck Grant, Paul Rogers, Walter Scott Gordon; Tipper, Guarnere, Rader, Heffron, Ranney, Johnny Martin, George Luz, Perconte, Jim Alley, and no less a personage than Burr Smith."

March 1982: "The Pennsylvania contingent got together at Dick Winters' place for a surprise party for Harry Welsh. Fenstermaker, Strohl, Guarnere, Guth had a great time."

1983: "Don Moone retired from the advertising business and now lives it up down in Florida. He and Gordon and Carwood Lipton had a reunion in New Orleans."

With only a couple of exceptions, these men had no

business or professional connections. None lived in the same town, few in the same state (except Pennsylvania). Yet they stayed in touch. In January 1981, Moone wrote Winters to thank him for a Christmas present and to fill him in: "It was great news that Talbert was finally located. I called him immediately and after an exchange of insults, we talked. I've always been fond of Tab. He took care of me in the old days. On New Year's Day at 6 A.M. my time, Tab called to wish me a good new year. He was bombed but coherent. He admits that he had a bottle problem as we suspected, but was 'on the wagon' except for special occasions. Guess New Year's Eve was one of those 'specials.'

"Don Malarkey called me at 3:00 A.M. on New Year's Eve morning and he too was well on his way."

Ranney retired to write poetry and his memoirs, but in September 1988 he died before he could get started.

Talbert was one of the few members of the company who just dropped out of sight. In 1980, Gordon enlisted the aid of his congressman and of George Luz's son Steve to locate Talbert. Ranney joined the search. Eventually they located him in Redding, California, and persuaded him to attend the 1981 company reunion in San Diego.

Ranney passed around his address. Winters and others wrote him. In his three-page handwritten reply to Winters, Talbert reminisced about their experiences. "Do you remember the time you were leading us into Carentan? Seeing you in the middle of that road wanting to move was too much! . . . Do you recall when we were pulling back in Holland? Lt. Peacock threw his carbine onto the road. He would not move. Honest to God I told him to retrieve the carbine and move or I would shoot him. He did as I directed. I liked him, he was a sincere and by the book officer, but not a soldier. As long as he let me handle the men he and I got along alright.

"Dick, this can go on and on. I have never discussed these things with anyone on this earth. The things we had are damn near sacred to me." He signed off, "Your Devoted Soldier forever."

Talbert had enclosed a recent photograph. He looked like a mountain man. In his reply, Winters told him to shave off the beard and get his hair cut if he intended to come to San Diego. He did, but he still showed up wearing tattered hunting clothes. The first morning, Gordon and Don Moone took him to a men's store and bought him new clothes. Before the year was out, he died.

Gordon wrote his epitaph. "Almost all of the men of Company E suffered wounds of various severity. Some of us limp, some have impaired vision or hearing, but almost without exception we have modified our lives to accommodate the injury. Tab continued in daily conflict with a demon within his breast. He paid a dear price for his service to his country. He could not have given more without laying down his life."

Dick Winters paid him the ultimate tribute: "If I had to pick out just *one* man to be with me on a mission in combat, it would be Talbert."

Talbert was the best, but he was one among many in the company who was respected for his qualities as a combat soldier. As Gordon notes, nearly every one of the men had been struck by the enemy—more than a hundred of the 180 were wounded, some twice, a few three times, one four times, while forty-eight of them had been killed. There was scarcely a survivor in the company whose life had not been saved by a comrade. All had given what they regarded as the best years of their lives to the war. As Dick Winters put it, "The result of sharing all that stress throughout combat has created a bond between the men of E Company that will last forever."

When I first interviewed Winters and three members of the company, Gordon, Carwood Lipton and Forrest Guth, it was 1988. We went through details of what the company did in Normandy. Moira had them stay for dinner, where I made a discovery. There was a closeness among them that was not quite unique in my quarter-century experience of interviewing veterans, but it surely was unusual. As they talked about other members of the company, about various reunions over the decades, it became obvious that they continued to be a band of brothers. Although they were scattered all across the North American continent and overseas, they knew each other's wives, children, grandchildren, each other's problems and successes. They visited regularly, kept in close contact by mail and by phone. They helped each other in emergencies and times of trouble. And the only thing they had in common was their three-year experiences in World War II, when they had been thrown together by the U.S. Army. I became intensely curious about how this remarkable closeness had developed. What I discovered was that they had all become, and remained, friends.

In one of his last newsletters, Mike Ranney wrote: "In thinking back on the days of Easy Company, I'm treasuring my remark to a grandson who asked, 'Grandpa, were you a hero in the war?'

" 'No,' I answered, 'but I served in a company of heroes.' "

This makes for a very special, lifelong friendship.

ELEVEN

Veterans

ON JUNE 7, 1981, I was at Pegasus Bridge, where the first action of D-Day took place. I was there with a group of American veterans and their wives, leading a tour of World War II battlefields. We had examined the bridge, marveled at the skill of the glider pilots who had landed smack beside the bridge with only moonlight for illumination, visited the small museum and cafe. I had just got the group back on the bus and was ready to move out—behind schedule, as usual—when a white-haired, exceedingly friendly older man, leaning on a cane, stopped me as I started to board the bus and asked, "I say, are any of you chaps from the British Sixth Airborne Division?"

"No, sir," I replied, "we're all Americans on this bus."

"Oh, I'm sorry," he said.

"Don't be sorry," I answered. "We're all rather proud to be Americans. Were you in the Sixth Airborne?"

"I was indeed," he replied. "I'm Major John Howard."

My God! I thought. Standing before me is the first company commander to go into action on D-Day, the man who has the opening scene in the movie *The Longest Day,* a man known all over the world for what he did in this place.

"How do you do? How do you do?" I exclaimed. I was pumping his hand. "What a thrill and honor to meet you."

He asked if "my chaps" would like to hear a word or two about what had happened here. Indeed they would, I assured him, and dashed into the bus to get everyone out. We gathered around Major Howard, who stood in the embankment, his back to the bridge. He told us what had happened in June 1944, and how, very vividly. The next year I had John as a featured speaker for another tour group, again in front of *his* bridge. He came again in 1983. As our bus pulled out that year heading for Rommel's headquarters on the Seine River on the way to Paris, Howard, standing in front of the cafe, snapped into a salute. At that moment I knew I wanted to write the story of Pegasus Bridge.

John agreed to give me all the time I needed and introductions to the surviving members of the company. Moira and I used my sabbatical to spend the fall semester in London, where I went out daily by train to different parts of England to do interviews. When I had finished, John told me I now had to go to Germany to meet Colonel Hans von Luck.

I said I didn't want to do that. I'd never been to Germany and never wanted to go. I knew no men who had fought for Germany in the Second World War and I never wanted to meet one. John said I had to go. Not only for the good of the book—Hans was in command of the panzer regiment that was charged with driving any British invaders at Pegasus Bridge into the sea, so his testimony was critical— but also because Hans was his dear friend and as fine a man as I would ever meet.

In Hamburg we met Hans and it changed some of my thinking. Fluent in six or seven languages, with aristocratic manners, a warm sense of humor and a marvelous ability to tell stories that catch you up and carry you along, partly because his technique was so good, mainly because the stories were so good. He spoke about his service with Rommel before the war, his experiences in Poland in 1939, France in 1940 (where his reconnaissance platoon was the first unit of

Rommel's division to reach the English Channel), the Russian campaign in 1941, the North Africa battles of 1942–43, then Normandy in 1944 and again on the eastern front after February 1945. He told about being in a POW camp in the Crimea for five years, working in coal mines.

I was a sort of Boswell to the two old soldiers. I was almost twenty years younger, young enough to have been their son. I had no combat experience, but I was writing this book. They told me what I needed to know. They liked that I cared and paid attention. I liked that they wanted to share their experiences with me.

Their willingness to share characterized the friendship between John and Hans. They met late in life, but they made up for the lost time through sharing and caring. They were so thoughtful of each other. Whenever John left the States he bought cartons of Luckies. John never smoked, but Hans was a two-or-three-pack-a-day man all his life, and John knew that Hans preferred the Luckies made in the U.S.A. Hans would bring John special coffees from his trips to Africa. They knew each other's favorite foods and drinks, nap habits, what the other man was reading, what trips he had planned. They could talk endlessly, about past, present or future. They talked about the war, especially June 6, 1944. They knew each other's families and kept up with the comings and goings.

Although their backgrounds were entirely different— aristocratic estate owner in East Prussia and a graduate of the German cadet school vs. a Cockney barrel-maker's son who came up from the ranks—they had much in common, beginning with the fact that they had given the best years of their lives over to making war. They never wanted to see another war. But they had seen what Hitler and totalitarianism meant, and they wanted freedom. So in politics they were conservative, strong supporters of Britain's and Germany's national defense forces and of NATO.

They worked together, indeed that is how they met. In

1975 the Swedish military academy began bringing its cadets to Normandy for a study of the battle. The Swedes were especially interested in bridges. Sweden has lots of rivers; if the Red Army were to invade, the Swedes would find themselves blowing, defending and attacking bridges. They knew a bit about Pegasus Bridge and wanted to know more. So they arranged to bring the two commanders—Hans and John—to talk to their cadets about their experiences on D-Day.

The old men loved it. The cadets loved it. The faculty was delighted. So the visit of the Swedish cadets to Pegasus Bridge became an annual thing, with Hans and John doing the lecturing. They complemented each other. They knew how to share the stage, deferring when it was called for, stepping up and sneaking up when that was called for. Hans would conclude by saying that had Hitler released his panzers in the middle of the night, as Hans wanted him to do, the Germans would have driven Howard's company into the sea. John would scoff at this and point with pride at what his company had done.

Each year they would put on their show for my World War II class at the University of New Orleans. One time a student, shaking with indignation, demanded to know how Hans ever could have fought for Hitler. When Hans protested that he had been a regular army officer since 1927, and never a Nazi or SS, the student began reciting the crimes of the German army. He was pointing his finger at Hans, nearly shouting, saying Hans must have known about this or that atrocity, almost hinting that Hans must have been involved.

It was at my urging that Hans wrote his memoirs, *Panzer Commander.* We spent a week in Innsbruck one summer going over his manuscript. At one point he stated that he knew nothing about the death camps. I leaned back on the sofa, looked him in the eye and said, "Hans, no one in America is ever going to believe that."

"But it is true," Hans said, and he went on to convince me that it was.

The student didn't know anything of Hans's denial and almost certainly would not have believed it.

I had seen Hans in similar situations and I knew he would take care of himself. He was sensitive about others' sensibilities with regard to the Germany of the Nazi regime. He was also sensitive to being accused of wrongdoing, but he kept those feelings to himself.

On this occasion John Howard stepped in. He spoke directly to the student, telling him he had no idea what he was talking about, that Hans was an honorable man and it was absurd to accuse him of criminal activity. He said those of us lucky enough to live in the democracies do not have the right to cast stones at those who were unlucky enough to be caught in a Nazi nation.

Dick Winters was there. He, too, spoke up in Hans's defense and lectured the student on what he didn't know about war. Winters is the subject of another book of mine, *Band of Brothers.* He had a lot in common with John and Hans, and when we had got them together they very quickly became close friends. They traveled together, corresponded, kept up. They came on my tours and to our conferences in New Orleans. So on this occasion it seemed natural for Dick to speak up—and for me to think, What a scene this is, here were two of the best company commanders in the Allied force, with elite companies, one British gliderborne and the other American airborne, rising to defend the good name of a high-ranking German officer in front of an audience of American students.

And the wonder was the friendship between this improbable trio. It was very special. It makes me look forward to getting really old; I think there is a good chance of getting into some extraordinary friendships with men I have not yet met. From the example of Hans, John and Dick, I know it can be rewarding, a friendship free of cant, of competition, of seeking advantage, a friendship rich in trust and recognition.

The friendship of these three was based on mutual admiration and respect. They each had held the most difficult and dangerous job in the world, a company commander in combat, and done so with distinction. When they talked, they transcended nationality and were simply comrades in arms. They were wiser than they had been as youngsters and more tolerant.

They had led good, productive lives, but much different. John, who was in combat for the shortest period of the three, was the worst smashed up, the result of a driving accident in England in the summer of 1944. He became a civil servant and lived a modest life, except on June 6 each year, when he would join his friend Hans at Pegasus Bridge. Dick became a farmer—he had promised himself on D-Day night that if he lived through this, he would find himself a quiet farm somewhere to spend the remainder of his life. In 1950 he found it, in central Pennsylvania where he became a successful animal food products importer. He still lives there.

Their friendship centered around their war memories. Their careers were so different, there was nothing much to talk about there. But, in fact, they shared a deep sense of satisfaction. It is said best by my son Hugh, who wrote an afterword to the paperback edition of *Citizen Soldiers,* an essay on what it was like for him to interview German veterans. At one point he observes: "In the years since the war, the relationship between the German and American veterans has flourished. On several occasions, the American and German veterans associations have held joint ceremonies to honor their fallen comrades." We attended one at Remagen Bridge on the fiftieth anniversary of its capture, where American and German veterans of the battle swapped stories and drank beer. Hugh goes on: "But more often individuals have met by chance on some former battlefield. During the ensuing conversation—which usually begins with 'What outfit were you with?'—they find that they have a lot in common. Both the American veterans and the former soldiers of the Wehrmacht enjoy celebrating their postwar accomplishments. Like all grandparents, both take great pride in having created a prosperous and safe country for their children and grandchildren. They also enjoy talking to others who were there. Only somebody who was there understands that a front-line soldier's war amounted to looking out after your friends while 'trying to get out of this dirty business alive.' "

Hugh tells the story of Corporal Hans Herbst and Sergeant Murray Shapiro, who had been involved in a costly firefight and damn near killed each other as each squad lost a number of men. They met in a cemetery and became friends. Hugh writes, "When I think about how much a soldier's comrades meant to him, I wonder how the veterans can ever put the past behind them. But the story reveals more than just two men swapping tales. It is the conversation of two men who have learned to forgive. The American soldier can take a great deal of credit for making that conversation possible. He fought hard to win the war. But every step of the way, he strove to create peace. Such a tribute is perhaps as fine as any old soldier could wish, especially when it comes from his former opponent. 'I only want to add,' said Herbst with a chuckle, 'that today when I am with Americans, we are friends. They tell me I am lucky to be alive. I tell them I'm lucky that they are such poor shots.' "

THEY WERE TOGETHER with me and a tour group on the fiftieth anniversary of D-Day. They were there in starring roles—the television crews couldn't get enough of them. Interviews with them were broadcast worldwide. Hans did a commentary for Larry King. Dick did some for NBC-TV. John was featured on every news broadcast from the United Kingdom. They loved it. They were so glad to see the other two get recognition, and had so much fun themselves it was just a joy to behold.

Maybe the last friendship is the best one. It is like being a grandparent. It is God's reward for having done your best.

TWELVE

Father and Son

I'VE WAITED UNTIL THE END to write about my friendship with my father. The joy of discovering male friendship is clearest in that friendship because it took a lifetime to appreciate it. A father is not a pal—he is the figure of authority and stability. For my part I was lucky that mine lived to see me into adulthood, and that together we found we shared interests and forged a genuine friendship.

Dr. Stephen Hedges Ambrose was above all else a public servant. My brothers and I never knew that—we found out only later. In the late 1980s, when I was fifty years old and living in Bay St. Louis, Mississippi, on the Gulf Coast and close to Interstate 10, near various places where many midwesterners came for a winter vacation, those from Lovington, Illinois, or Whitewater, Wisconsin, where my father had been a general practitioner of medicine from the early thirties to 1963, would see my name in a local phone book and drop in for a quick visit.

Always, they wanted to tell me what a great man my father was. No one else in the world except his patients knew that—he never made a lot of money, or invented a new drug, or pioneered in medicine, or taught a young genius, or had done anything worthy of note. But old women would tell me, "He delivered my children and grandchildren." Usually in the middle of the night, at the patient's home. After a 12:30 A.M. or a 2 A.M. phone call, he would dress and then drive out to the patient's farm, relying on the compass he had on his dashboard to keep him headed straight. And her husband would show me a finger and say, "Doc sewed that on for me." Inquiry would reveal that the patient had lost his finger in a combine or tractor accident. I would ask how much Dad charged. "A dollar per stitch," the farmer would say, beaming.

Some of the visitors would be middle-aged, graduates of the local university (then Whitewater State Teachers College, now the University of Wisconsin Whitewater), where Dad served as doctor, treating the students without charge, sometimes in his office, sometimes at our home, sometimes in their dorm room, always without pay. They, too, thought of him as the finest doctor there ever was.

So do I. When as an eleven-year-old boy I had rheumatic fever, a heart disease that often kills, he kept me in bed all summer and fixed it—just as he always fixed everything. I know farmers who had not just fingers but toes, ears, noses and other body parts sewn on successfully by my dad. I know women who were delivered by Dad whose children and grandchildren he also delivered.

But to me in childhood he was less a saint or hero, more an ordinary guy with too many faults. He approved of nothing that I did, disapproved of almost everything, and let me know in a loud voice where and how I had let him down. As he was also strikingly handsome, soft-spoken (generally) and a volunteer doctor for the high school football team on which my brothers and I played—his responsibility included examining some thirty boys to make sure they were fit for the sport and being at every game to treat their injuries—I could be nothing but respectful to him.

Still, none of his public service made much difference to me. I wanted him to be like the other fathers in town, with plenty of toys and encouragement for his boys. It wasn't like that in the Ambrose household. If we wanted to ice-skate, we learned by ourselves. So, too, if we wanted to hunt, or play basketball or football. If we wanted to watch TV we went to a neighbor's, at least until 1952, when he finally got a tiny set.

But if we wanted to be big men—honest, trustworthy, capable of doing what we said we were going to do—why, we imitated him.

BECAUSE HE WAS BUSY growing his income (which he never did to any considerable degree) he had little time for his boys. For our part, we respected him as an officer in the Navy, a doctor, a man everyone in town admired, the man our mother, Cee Cee, worshipped. Like many of the men of his time and place he was a stern disciplinarian with impossible-to-reach standards. From the day that we moved into our new house he put us boys to work mowing the lawn, shoveling the walks and weeding the garden, which meant every grass blade cut and swept up, all the walks free of snow of any kind, and every weed—but no vegetables—removed from the garden. Further, we should study in school. He insisted that we get straight As, that we take Latin, learn to type, play an instrument in the band and participate in all the extracurricular activities, including sports. He was old-fashioned in every way, including keeping up the lawn, the hedges, the trees, the garden and the driveway in the approved and finest manner possible—which meant we had to work harder. We did it all, and today we agree among ourselves that these were the best things we ever did.

We had his guidance, complete and without question, as long as we did what we were told, but what we never felt we had was his friendship. Whitewater in the late forties and early fifties was an ideal place for fishing and hunting pheasants, rabbits, ducks and geese, but we did those things on our own or with our classmates. In high school we played football, basketball and track, and Dad would come to the games, not so much to see us play as to be present in the event that someone got hurt. He didn't much care about how well we did in sports—our mother, who never missed a game, did—but he always insisted that we took the toughest academic classes and did well in them.

Except for his medical journals, he seldom read. Cee Cee read constantly, historical romances that she got out of the library. With no encouragement from either of them or from my brothers, I spent much of my time in the local Carnegie Library, reading history books, especially about Napoleon, Washington, Jefferson and Lincoln. Mother and Dad had a casual interest in Wisconsin history and on occasion I'd get them to take me to historical sites.

From the time we moved to Wisconsin, we lived for the first summer at the log cabin on our own pond, without electricity, in northern Wisconsin with Mother, who had inherited eighty acres and the cabin from her father (by 1945 a dead U.S. Army colonel who had no extra money to pass along) while Dad did the carpentry to restore the house in Whitewater. He would come to the cabin for weekends; otherwise we had no car (or phone, not to mention electricity). We all loved it, beyond words. Dad went there each fall for deer season. From the time I was fourteen years old he would take me with him. Often we would go with a group of hunters, who were all veterans. That was one of the great experiences because among many other things, I got to hear them talk about the war. Those were my first war stories, and enthralling. (I played pickup basketball with a bunch of ex-GIs—GI Bill students at the local college, living near us—but they never talked about the war.)

As I got ready to graduate from high school, in 1953 at age seventeen, Dad very much wanted me to major in pre-medicine and then go on to the University of Wisconsin medical school and finally take up his practice in Whitewater. This seemed like a reasonable and logical choice to me. He also wanted me to pledge his fraternity, Psi U, and live in the Psi U house.

At the cabin that summer I promised my father that I would do what he wanted. He was as pleased at this news as I had ever seen him.

But none of it happened. Psi U had no spaces available in the fraternity house, so I joined Chi Psi, which did have a room available in what they called their Lodge. Dad was greatly disappointed. He never approved of Chi Psi. We were now past the point when he would kick or spank me, so he let me know how he felt verbally. I had promised, and he had told my mother and a few of his friends. Now he was humiliated. Still, it was my life and I could lead it the way I wanted—but my way wasn't his.

Even though I was still in pre-med, the decision turned out to be the beginning of my scholar's life. In my sophomore year I took a course in American history required by the University of Wisconsin, even for pre-meds. My professor was the renowned William B. Hesseltine, a superb teacher. He told us that in his course we would be doing research on a Wisconsin nineteenth-century figure, writing up his or her biography, making him or her into a subject to be included in the dictionary of Wisconsin biography he was working up for the State Historical Society. Instead of just repeating what we had learned in three or four books (as we did in other courses), he said, we would be doing original research and adding to the sum of the world's knowledge.

The words caught me up. It had never before occurred to me that I could do such a thing as add to the sum of the world's knowledge. At the end of that lecture I went up to Professor Hesseltine and told him that I wanted to do what he did for a living, and asked, "How do I do that?"

He laughed and replied, "Stick around and I'll show you."

Right after, I went down to the registrar and told him that I wanted to switch to a history major. He said that was fine with him, so long as I wanted to go on to graduate school in history. Fine with me, I said.

That evening I called my dad to tell him what I had decided. He was angry, hurt, disappointed. I told him what a great man Professor Hesseltine was. He grunted. I now realize he must have felt that as I had chosen another older man to be my leader, I had rejected him. But he didn't say that. Instead he took a breath and said I could do whatever I wanted to do.

My brothers didn't help much. They, too, found premed to be not to their liking, all that chemistry, physics and the like. Harry went to Dartmouth, where he, too, rejected Psi U and majored in business. Bill came to Wisconsin, where he joined Chi Psi and majored in accounting. That left Dad without a successor.

I stayed at Madison through the next three years of my undergraduate work. I went home to Whitewater and lived with my parents through the summer, as I worked to make some spending money. I also talked to Dad about the Civil War and got him interested. He, too, began reading—after all, his grandfather was in the war and he had been born and raised in Illinois, the home of many famous regiments and of Abraham Lincoln. In the summer of my junior year I very much wanted to take a couple of weeks to see some Civil War battlefields. I was determined to ride my bike to Shiloh, in southern Tennessee, where U. S. Grant had his first battle. One of Dad's patients was a truck driver who was on his way to New Orleans, and Dad arranged for me to ride with him to near Shiloh. I slept on the battlefield and rode all around it. After I rode back to Wisconsin, I had several long discussions with Dad about what I had seen and experienced.

The next summer he suggested and I agreed that we take a drive down to Springfield, Illinois, to see Lincoln's home there. I'll never forget the trip. We had both read Carl Sandburg's biography and two or three others. We talked Lincoln the whole way. I told Dad on that trip that Mr. Lincoln had made me believe in God because Abraham Lincoln could not just have died, that he had to be up in heaven somewhere. My father, who never talked about religion with me or anyone else, replied that he agreed with me. We went on down to Mississippi to visit Vicksburg, where we saw all the sights and then went to the magnificent Illinois monument, where my great-grandfather had his name on the wall. (Many years later I reprinted in an article on Vicksburg, in *American History Illustrated* magazine, a letter my great-grandfather had written his wife on July 4, 1863—the day Vicksburg surrendered to Grant. This greatly pleased my father.)

By this time it was clear to me that he knew more about the Civil War than I did. On his own, he had embraced my interest and read deeply about the war. His new-found support of what I was doing was the most important thing in my life. Dad became a founder of the Civil War Round Table in Madison (still an ongoing organization; I have spoken to it many times in the ensuing five decades, until the 1980s with Dad in the audience). He became a friend of Professor Hesseltine. And we spent much time at various Civil War sites.

I was now hooked on the American Civil War, and beyond that on American history generally. My father was, too.

And he was the only friend I had who was. He knew what it meant to me; I was overjoyed that it meant so much to him, thanks to my interest. He loved the subject as much as I did, and neither of us could ever see any reason for me to have any other profession. He had not just resigned himself to my doing what I did, but he participated in my life's work with me and grew as I did.

As I began visiting World War II battlefields, he was always willing to come along, even though I went to Europe, never to the Pacific where he had served. Together Dad and I went to Omaha Beach, to Utah Beach, to the Battle of the Bulge and to many other World War II sites. Together we visited his great-great-great-grandfather's grave in Chilton-Foliat in central England. In his own way, and without ever insisting on it, he made me into an historian, something I'll never be able to repay him for. Just as he became my friend—in some ways my closest friend in my adult years.

He had always been somewhat rigid, insisting that his boys do as they were told and toe the line. I was keenly, gratefully aware that he had made an exception for my embrace of history. By the late sixties, after his boys had all left home and graduated from college and were making their own living, Dad took care of the odd jobs that we boys had done around home (it would be a disgrace for any man to hire out such work).

But he did not overcome his prejudices against women working. My mother, Cee Cee, was desperate to work in anything that she found interesting that came her way. He said absolutely no. The wife of the town doctor was not going to work at anything. He wouldn't have it. Cee Cee drank too much, smoked too much, had too many friends and was deeply involved in local politics, including being an elected member of the Walworth County Board and the

Whitewater School Board. He didn't really approve, but allowed it.

Finally, in 1974, he allowed Mother to work in the travel agency next door to his office. They could drive to work and home again together. She loved it. A veteran traveler, she had planned many trips she never got to take (because Dad had a patient who was sick or who was pregnant and due to deliver on the date she had picked), but still she made Dad come with her on some trips to this place or that, which to the people of Whitewater seemed exotic.

That my mother should do whatever my father said seemed entirely natural to me; that she should not work seemed entirely normal, as for the life of me I couldn't see why she needed either the experience or the money. But she was great at the job and much appreciated by the owners of the business. One day that summer, 1975, however, she returned from lunch, hung up her jacket, announced "I'm back" and fell down, dead. The others in the office rushed next door to get Dad, who came, examined her and could do nothing (he later blamed himself for her death).

I was working on a book about Crazy Horse and Custer that summer and was camping out in Wyoming with my family. That evening a state trooper pulled up to our tent and escorted me over to a farmhouse that had a telephone. I called home, as instructed by the policeman, and talked to Dad, who gave me the news I couldn't believe. I protested that I had just seen Mother a month before and she had been in good health. He assured me it was true, and that the funeral would be in three days. So in the morning I packed up Moira, the kids and the dog, and we set out in our VW bus for Wisconsin, where we arrived two days later. Dad had seen a lot of death in his lifetime, and he didn't show how this one affected him. My brothers flew to Chicago and came to

Whitewater, and like me they were more or less devastated by Cee Cee's death. Somehow we all got through the funeral and the burial. Harry and Bill flew home. Moira, the kids and I took Dad up to our cabin.

I could never get him to cry. When I asked him why, on the trip or at the cabin, he replied that crying was just feeling sorry for yourself. I said that was just silly, I had interviewed many wives of veterans who told me they had cried for their husbands when they got the telegraph from the War Department, and that their tears seemed to me to be entirely appropriate. He said that such tears were for women only.

We had a pretty good week together, fishing, hiking, driving through the woods. I couldn't see any change in him brought on by the death of the only woman he had ever loved. We spent much time talking about American wars and American history generally, as we always did. We never talked about my mother, although I wanted to, for many obvious reasons, but most of all because I lived at this cabin with her and my brothers in the summer of 1946 and had many memories. But he just would not allow it.

Then, after a week or so, Moira went down to the pier to peel some apples. The bluegill gathered under her, to eat the apple peels she was depositing into the lake. This was one of my mother's favorite things to do at the cabin. Dad took one look and began to weep. It was the first time I'd ever seen him cry. He insisted that we go back to Whitewater the next day so that he could go back to work.

He worked until he died. During his final illness, cancer, I would fly to Chicago fairly frequently to rent a car and drive to Whitewater for a visit, as would my brothers. But in his last few weeks it was Moira who was there constantly, a companion, someone to cook and clean up for him, a steadfast friend. He died in 1983. He was my first and always most important friend. I didn't learn that until the end, when he taught me the most important thing, that the love of father-son-father-son is a continuum, just as love and friendship are expansive.

About the Author

STEPHEN E. AMBROSE is the author of numerous books of history, including *Citizen Soldiers, Undaunted Courage* and *D-Day,* as well as biographies of Dwight D. Eisenhower and Richard Nixon. He lives in Bay St. Louis, Mississippi, and Helena, Montana.